THE ENCHANTING
FRENCH RIVIERA

Text by
JEAN MATHÉ

Translated by
EVELYN ROSSITER

minerva

© 1995, Éditions Minerva SA, Genève (Suisse)

CONTENTS

HYÈRES AND THE GIENS PENINSULA

Hyères is truly the gateway to the French Riviera.

Two and a half miles from the sea, in a tranquil setting with an exceptionally mild climate, renowned throughout Europe, it was so fashionable as a winter resort in the eighteenth and nineteenth centuries that its guests included Tolstoy and Queen Victoria.

Situated on a fertile plain ideally suited for crops, fruit and flowers, it is most particularly an oasis of market gardening. The modern part of the town which Mistral thought of as "the garden of the Hesperides" is quiet and uncluttered. Open space and gardens are plentiful along its broad avenues which are lined with splendid palm trees. The new town manages never to be overly bustling: it is a serene place which has preserved a faintly seedy old-fashioned charm.

The old part of the town, clustered below the ruins of the castle, is situated at the top of Castéou Hill, which rises over 600 ft. A pleasant walk is to be had from the church of Saint-Louis.

At Hyères: a square in the old town (top) and the castle (bottom). Two views of Giens (facing page).

Like so many places of worship built in the pure Romanesque style of the twelfth century, it was enlarged and remodeled in the fifteenth and sixteenth centuries in the Gothic mode. Later restorations left it with neither style nor personality.

The main axis of the old town is Rue Massillon, which ends at the square named in honor of the great man of Hyères, Jean-Baptiste Massillon (1663-1742). The famous preacher, of whom Louis XIV said: "Whenever I hear him I feel dissatisfied with myself", was born nearby, at 7, Rue Rabaton. A lively, colorful and picturesque market, replete with its own aromas, is held on this square, in the shadow of the Saint-Blaise tower, formerly part of a residence of the Knights Templar, built in 1200. The Romanesque church of Saint-Paul, a dark, forbidding fortress of the faith, towers over the rooftops of the old town from its vantage point on a square some distance uphill. Though built in the eleventh century, it was altered beyond recognition by a succession of remodelings. It has retained, however, its gloomy nave, a reminder of the time when it was really nothing but a heavily fortified chapel, with only the tiniest openings.

Beyond lies the tangle of steep, narrow, winding streets, in which light and shade play along the façades. The most interesting streets have old-fashioned, evocative names, such as Rue Sainte-Claire, Saint-Pierre, Saint-Bernard, Paradis or Bar-

bacane. A stroll takes us past some Romanesque or Renaissance houses and through the ancient gates, named Princes, Souquette, Fenouillet and Baruc, in the town ramparts, which long ago ceased to perform any defensive role: nowadays they merely enclose some dilapidated sections of the once awe-inspiring castle, where Saint Louis spent a few days in 1254 on his way back from the Crusade.

Next to the old walls is the handsome Château Saint-Bernard, formerly the residence of the Comtesse de Noailles, surrounded by terraced gardens which lead up to the district of Saint-Paul. From here there is a splendid view of the plain, where fruit and palm trees grow alongside mimosas, alternating with fields of cultivated flowers such as violets, wallflowers and roses. Painters and artists have always been attracted by the local climate: Paul Bourget used to spend every winter at the Plantier estate, and Michelet died there in 1874. The curious Olbius Riquier exotic gardens contain all the Mediterranean species found in the region.

The Giens Peninsula was formed by an accumulation of coastal silt which has linked Giens Island to the coast by two parallel strips of land. The western strip, starting at Almanarre, is so low that it can scarcely be seen at all from the sea, whereas a broad highway runs along the eastern spur, past the Pesquiers salt marshes, and providing some highly unusual views which are even unique along this part of the coast. The houses of the village of La Capte and then La Bergerie, looking out over the large beach on the eastern shore of the peninsula, are scattered among the pine groves which hold its sand securely in place.

The small town of Giens, which Charles II gave to his personal physician, by the name of Ortolan, in 1254, stands in the middle of the former island. Giens has a number of features which make the detour worthwhile–the ruins of Pontèves Castle, which tower over some very old streets and lend it a slightly feudal air, as well as some fine walks which may be taken in the vicinity; but it is the islands which visitors really came to see.

THE HYERES ISLANDS

At one time they were known as the Golden Isles (Iles d'Or), a name which they were given during the Renaissance, apparently on account of the glistening reflections of their micaschists in the setting sun.

In actual fact the rocks themselves are barely visible, being hidden by lush vegetation. But they are also

very sunny islands, attracting substantial numbers of vacationers to their beaches, which are sheltered from the mistral and shaded from the sun by umbrella pines.

Boats leave from the Fondue tower, an old Saracen fort renovated by Richelieu in the seventeenth century, where cars have to be left behind, as the islands are reserved for pedestrians and cyclists. On the way across one can think back to the history of these islands.

The Greeks called them Stoechades, which contains the roots of various words: «string of beads», «alinement» and «lavender» (stoechas). For them it was a port of call on their shipping routes, and also a center for the collection of the

Porquerolles: view from Fort Agathe (facing page) and the harbor (below). Left: the Golden Isle shaded by umbrella pines.

murex, a once valuable shellfish which was very abundant along these coasts, and from which purple dye was extracted.

On the seaward side, these islands, which are really detached fragments of the Maures Massif, whose geological features they reproduce, are bordered by sheer cliffs. The beaches and the jetties are on the north shore, facing the coast. Visitors pursue a single purpose when they come here: nature. The sun and the moist sea air sustain a micro-climate well suited to the lush vegetation which is one of the chief attractions of these islands.

On account of their poor, rocky soil, ill-suited to crops, and the lack of fresh water, they have never been settled for any length of time, especially as their remoteness and low

contours (525 ft maximum) made them an easy prey for invaders.

The Greeks and Phoceans were followed by Roman settlers, who established short-lived farming operations. In the fifth century the monks of Lérins resumed the effort by trying to attract farmers and fishermen to the islands. After yet another failure the islands became a base of operations for Saracen and Barbary pirates from the seventh to the sixteenth centuries. In 1531 François I restored and built fortifications to make them easier to defend, and devised the noble title of «Marquis des Iles d'Or», which he conferred on his friend Bertrand d'Ornezan, a general of galleys. Fifteen years later Charles V took possession, turning the territory into a «Duchy of the Isles of Austria», for

the Genoese admiral Andrea Doria. Yet in 1536 the famous Turkish corsair Barbarossa, who happened to be an ally of France, used the islands as shelter for his fleet.

Henri II, restoring French control, gave the marquisate to a German, Christoph von Roquendorf. The prime necessity of the day was to find people willing to live on the islands. The French kings exempted their inhabitants from payment of taxes and also established a penal colony there. However, these strange settlers, far from opposing the seasonal pirates active in the area, simply made things worse.

Eventually Louis XIV expelled the convicts. Once the marquisate had become vacant the land was sold, in 1785, to various private individuals.

In order to prevent a tourist inva-

sion, the State turned Port-Cros into a national park; in 1971 it bought Porquerolles, thereby saving it from the clutches of real estate speculators.

Porquerolles was known to the Greeks as Protea. Its tiny harbor, surrounded by a scattered hamlet of white and pink houses, half submerged in mimosas, tamarisks and eucalyptus, is still dominated by the Sainte-Agathe fort, built in the sixteenth century to protect the roadsteads from pirate raids. The chapel of Sainte-Anne (1850) is scarcely more attractive than those military memories. Visitors go to Porquerolles for one reason: it is a superb walking country, in the midst of magnificent vegetation.

To the south the lighthouse stands on a schist cliff 295 ft above the sea. In the east are beaches: La Courtade,

Porquerolles: the village church (facing page), the fort at Petit Langoustier (above), and a creek in the Estérel (left).

13

and Notre-Dame, beneath the sixteenth century Alicastre fort, which legend identifies as the den of a mythical monster and where, according to tradition, the Man in the Iron Mask paused briefly on his way to the island of Sainte-Marguerite. To the west are the forests of the Grand and the Petit Langoustier, and Argent beach, its micaschists glinting in the sun.

Port-Cros, known to the Greeks as Mese, is the most mountainous island, in the center of the group.

Originally in the hands of the Ligurians, cleared for farming by the monks of Lérins in the fifth century, then devastated by the Moors and later by the Turks, it had to wait until 1963 before being made a national park.

The coastline is deeply indented, and the water is so pure that you can see down 130 ft. Besides being a paradise of nature, Port-Cros is also an outstanding place for nature walks, such as the botanical trail and

the beach of La Palud, La Sardinière farm, Port-Man Point, and Solitude Valley.

Levant Island, a long rocky strip of land (five miles by just over half a mile), is better known for its nudist colony than for any feature of real interest: visitors are usually of the kind that seek a total sun-tan. Two-thirds of the island are occupied by the French Navy (1,500 out of a total of 2,500 acres), which allows no visitors at all to enter the eastern part. Vegetation is poor and stunted. The hermits of the early years of Christianity were replaced by the monks of Lérins and later by the Benedictines. It was a penitentiary in the eighteenth century and until 1866, before receiving its nudist visitors, at the appropriately named Heliopolis («Sun City»).

On the way back from the islands we once again pass through Giens, but then, avoiding Hyères, we follow the coast as far as Port-Pothuau, before connecting with the national

highway running along the Hyères salt marshes.

At La Londe a narrow but delightfully rustic road leads to the village of Cabasson—whose name derives from the Provençal word for fish bait– opposite the fort at Brégançon.

In 118 a Roman fort already existed on this isolated rock. The present citadel, which for the most part dates from the time of Louis XIV, was home to Joan the Mad, wife of Philippe II, in 1348; Spinola and his gang of brigands from 1387 to 1406; and Charles IX in 1564. Henri III elevated this fortified rock to the ludicrous status of a marquisate, while Napoleon gave it its definitive identity as a powerful fortress in the Provençal style. Ever since it became the summer residence of the Presidents of the Republic, it has been connected to the mainland by a dike nearly 500 ft long.

Having returned to the national highway, and before reaching Le Lavandou, we can make a side-trip to Cap Bénat and Gaou Bay, which nestles in a setting of pines and garrigues. This rugged and deeply-indented section of the coast, with alternating sandy or pebbly beaches and inlets, is a fine introduction to the flower-laden shores of Le Lavandou.

Views of Port-Cros (above and right) and the Ile du Levant (left).

LE LAVANDOU AND THE MAURES COAST

Le Lavandou, whose name, according to the romantics, derives from lavender, while linguists see in it a form of the Latin verb «to wash».

It consists of a beautiful beach of fine sand and a pleasant, well-sheltered harbor, from which fishing boats have long been ousted by pleasure craft. This place has changed a great deal since it was made famous in the

last century by the musician Ernest Rey, known as Reyer, before his death in 1909. Renoir moved here in 1891, and Pouguy in 1927; Nicolas de Stael (1911-55) painted some of his most famous canvases at Le Lavandou. Since then its charm has been somewhat tarnished by the hordes of summertime visitors and by urban sprawl, replete with dull, now prematurely aged office blocks and lifeless vacation communities.

A short distance outside Le Lavandou, the Maures massif edges closer to the sea. From quite high up the road follows these geological contortions, passing a series of fairly well-known seaside resorts.

Despite its excellent beach, Saint-Clair is the most modest of these, and the most popular. Two painters, Cross (1856-1910) and Van Rysselberghe (1862-1926), lived here until their deaths. The tiny beach at La

Fossette lies hidden within a deep inlet. Aiguebelle, taking advantage of its situation on a loop in the highway, has developed as a small, quiet resort.

Cavalière, however, is the star attraction along this section of the coast, which is one of the most beautiful parts of the Corniche. Its broad, harmoniously proportioned beach of fine sand, well sheltered from the mistral at the mouth of the cool Hubac Bleu Valley, far from the highway, which at this point swings inland, stretches for nearly five thousand feet between Layet Point and Cap Nègre, which was stormed on 15 August 1944 by Allied troops. On the other hand, Pranousquier («the monastery of the meadow») consists of villas scattered over hillsides covered with pines and holm-oaks. Formerly a free port of the Carthusian monastery of La Verne, it is now a

small but pleasant beach. Canadel-sur-Mer (from the word for reed) nestles snugly in a fold of the last slopes of the Pradel hills.

The ravine in which Le Rayol is situated, however, is probably the most superb along the Corniche. It lies in a natural amphitheater covered with vegetation, cut in two by the highway. The downhill section is blanketed with an astonishing profusion of vegetation–pines and eucalyptus growing among clematis and wild convolvulus. A number of delightful rural lanes lead to villas nestling in the midst of this floral paradise, which descends in tiers as far as the beach. In the 1920s Le Rayol was a highly fashionable resort.

Further uphill we come to the much drier Val de Beauté; here the vegetation consists of aloes and cactuses, which climb the slope from

The beach at Le Lavandou (facing page). View of Le Rayol (above).

The yacht harbor at Cavalaire.

one terrace to the next up to a superb belvedere situated in front of a small chapel.

Then the road swings away from the coast and winds its way around the massive Chappe Point, passing through much steeper and more rugged terrain. This part of the coast, which is known as the Pradel Corniche, is quite wild and virtually lacking in houses, as the slope is too steep. There are hardly any structures at all on the innumerable headlands which jut out into the sea, thickly carpeted with their curly, dark green garrigues, along the whole of the Maures coastline.

Here the road is situated halfway up the slope, between the towering granite abutments of the Pradel mountains and the whimsical outline of the shore, looking out towards the Levant Islands, which lie at anchor across the bay like some giant petrified fleet. Eventually the road becomes less tortuous, and descends towards the sea, reaching Cavalaire at the west end of a huge bay stretching between Cap Cavalaire and Cap Lardier.

The sandy beach, which is the biggest along the Maures coastline, extends for two and a half miles against the backdrop of the Pradel mountains. It was this feature of the terrain which caused it to be chosen, first by the Phenicians, who colonized it as a port of call along their maritime routes—one in which their boats were pulled onto the sand each evening; and later by the Counts of Grimaud, who used this site to build watchtowers and forts; and lastly by the Allies for their landing in August 1944.

Various views of the Corniche des Maures.

greatly softened by numerous eucalyptus trees, and especially mimosas.

No trace now remains of the proud Gaulish hamlet which was home to the Bormani tribe at the time of Caesar's arrival in these parts. Looking around at this enchanting village, one finds it hard to imagine that its history since the departure of the

BORMES-LES-MIMOSAS AND ITS MOUNTAIN

The Maures Massif, a powerful block of crystalline schists, similar to the Auvergne and the Armorique, is one of the most ancient geological formations in France.

At a very early stage its gneiss and granite bedrock was reshaped to form a real mountain, though its altitude of 1,640 ft is in fact rather modest.

Covered with a thick fleece of pine, holm oak and *garrigue*, it is also home to a number of exotic species, such as orange, lemon, eucalyptus and mimosa, which were introduced here in the nineteenth century.

The combination of forests and sunshine, in a summer climate which is absolutely dry, makes the massif a traditional victim of the fires which rage across it each year. In these parts fire is a dreaded scourge.

The name Maures derives from *Maouro*, a Provençal word meaning "dark wood", though this same etymology includes an allusion to the Arabs, or Moors who came from Spain and wrought havoc along the coast from the eighth to the tenth centuries. This constant insecurity compelled the inhabitants, who made their living from the tiny fishing harbors dotted along the coast, to build the picturesque "perched villages" which are among the chief attractions of the region.

Clinging to the tops of sheer rocky spurs, they provided a magnificent vantage point from which it was easy to see the approach of the enemy, while at the same time serving as a safe refuge when the marauders came ashore. One consequence of this state of affairs was their considerable economic isolation. Moreover, even after the disappearance of Moors and pirates, security was still poor, due to the depredations of local outlaws. Although it was of a different variety, this brand of insecurity remained widespread until the last century troughout this splendid scenic terrain.

Bormes-les-Mimosas, which is spread out over the first slopes of the massif, at an altitude of 525 ft, enjoys an exceptional location, set in a ring of hills with a full southerly exposure, and protected by wooded high ground, at the edge of the Dom Forest, from the gusts of the mistral.

For that very reason this most amazing floral paradise has become a world-famous winter resort. The harshness of the mountain terrain is

Romans has been one long succession of disasters: it was ravaged by the Saracens in 730, looted by Barbary or Turkish pirates in 1393 and 1529, then decimated by the plague in 1482 and laid waste by the Spanish armies of Charles V in 1539. Having survived these calamities, Bormes was, until the Revolution, a free, independent city, administered by a Council of Elders whose democratic voting procedures involved the use of balls made of cork, a commodity which is abundant throughout the region.

What used to be the center of Bormes in medieval time is now the Place de la Liberté, in the upper section of the town. It includes the chapel of Saint-François, a Gothic structure of the sixteenth century, surrounded by an old cemetery with cypress trees. In front of the church a recent statue (1870) of Saint-François-de-Paul perpetuates the memory of this saint, who is said to have saved the village from the plague.

A delightful network of quaint cobble-stoned streets, which are in places so steep that one of them is called *Rompi cuou*, or "break neck", are the major attraction of this village, which is situated in the midst of such exceptional vegetation that one finds it difficult to tell whether it consists of houses framed by a bouquet, or a perched village hidden among the gardens. Here, at any rate, the colors and scents matter as much as ancient stone, particularly in winter, when the soft teeming mass of yellow mimosas stands out brightly against the blue sky and fills the streets with perfume.

A number of passes–Landon, Barral and Le Canadel–lead us to the discovery of magnificent scenery, both along the coast and inland. There is no more rewarding route that one can take in the mountain landscape around Bormes.

LES MAURES

Above Bormes the increasingly winding road climbs to the Caguo-Ven pass, which despite its grand airs, levels out at the modest altitude of 780 ft.

The Chartreuse de La Verne: ruins (below) and historic buildings (facing page).

On the way up it bypasses the chapel of Notre-Dame-de-Constance, which, though founded in the twelfth century, was so extensively remodelled that it has retained nothing of its original beauty. Perched on a rocky spur at 1,025 ft, it provides a peerless vantage point.

Things have certainly changed in these parts since Maupassant, who was fascinated by the harshness and the beauty of the local terrain, and described it as "an incredibly wild landscape, without roads, villages or houses." Yet as soon as we move away from the sea, we enter a world of trees and winds, bristling with aloes and Barbary figs, where even the mistral seems to become tamer, slowing its pace and soaking up the fragrances which abound in the warm air. The sea is always close at hand, in the background at the mouth of each valley, embroidering the wooded hills which come down to meet it with its perpetual blue and white trim.

In the very middle of the massif, we come to the archetypical simple and quiet village. Collobrières, situated in a small sedimentary basin, is so far from the coast that it can expect to remain forgotten.

Today it strikes one as a quiet sleepy place which has retained the slightly seedy charm of those more modest climatic resorts which have remained apart from the frantic migrations of summer. Its large square, with its heavy stone benches, is shaded by centuries-old plane trees. Its old houses look down on the humble stream which flows through it, and which is far less majestic than its name–Réal ("royal") Collobrier–would seem to suggest. Here everything is peaceful, lazy and relaxed. As it does not depend on the tourist business for its livelihood, the village has wisely chosen to focus on specialized craftsmanship relying on local raw materials, making preserved fruits, glazed chestnuts and natural cork.

Visitors should take care not to miss the turn off the fine forest road which leads to the ruins of the Chartreuse de Verne. Few natural settings are as majestic as this. At an altitude of 1,360 ft, on a wide platform which very much resembles a monastic tonsure in the midst of the forest of chestnut trees, the remains of the Chartreuse, in this wild and forgotten landscape, await their visitors. Maupassant and Paul Arène devoted some exceedingly lyrical pages to this remarkable building.

There can be few ruins which are so pathetic in their desolation, and at the same time so romantic as the ruins of this out-of-the-way monastery.

This younger sister of the Chartreuse de Montrieux, north of Toulon, used to occupy a much larger area, as a small structure which the monks used as an observatory can still be seen more than 600 yards from the monastic buildings.

It was built in 1170, at the joint request of the bishops of Toulon and Fréjus, most probably on the site of a Roman temple to Diana–a goddess who must have been drawn quite naturally to the beauty of this forest.

Rebuilt after two accidental fires, it was looted during the wars of religion. It ceased to function as a monastery after the revolutionary authorities had banished its monks to Italy and sold off its furniture. It was placed on the register of historic monuments in 1921 and bought by the State in 1961, but is still very much a ruin.

Its monumental porch is embellished with green serpentine. This marvellous material, much often used for frames or decorative motifs, brightened the brown schist of the walls. The doorway leads into the inner courtyard. The monastery is

solidly fortified. Visitors are received opposite the entrance, in the middle of the main building, which consists of a splendid vaulted twelfth century kitchen, and a bakery built in the sixteenth. The part of the Chartreuse that has been best preserved–a chapel, a charming little cloister, also of green serpentine, and a restored refectory in which local products are now served–is situated behind this guest house. The large cloister looking out over the gardens, with the monks' cells opening onto it, is, however, entirely ruined. The same is true of an old windmill, situated outside the monastic enclosure.

The silence and the solitude of these ruins are disturbed only by the eternal plaintive wind blowing through the chestnut trees on the side of the hill.

There can be no doubt that the ravages of time have in no way diminished the mystic power of the stone of these ruins, which are perhaps even more impressive now than they were when the Chartreuse was in its heyday.

The familiar silhouette of the perched village of Grimaud–one of the most remarkable specimens of its kind in Provence–can be seen from a long way off. In its superb location, high on an outcropping of rock, its houses cling to the slope between the Giscle valley and the imposing ruins of its castle. It has a very proud bearing even today, and is unquestionably one of the most spectacular villages of its kind in the Maures.

The Arabs then moved in along the coast, establishing Fraxine (Lagarde-Freinet) as a Saracen capital, and retaining it until 973 as a Moorish outpost. Freed by Guillaume, the first Count of Provence, the hamlet and its small territory became a barony offered to Gibalin de Grimaldi, a driving force behind the Provençal "Reconquest" of the coast from the infidels. His successor, who was known as Grimaldus, was the one who built the fortress. The new village took his name, Grimaud, in memory of the House of Grimaldi.

Today the castle is unfortunately very much a ruin, not open to the public because of the danger that parts of it may actually collapse. There remains an old quarter surrounding the church square, where we find the main buildings which have survived since the Middle Ages. A Romanesque basilica of the eleventh century (1087) dedicated to St Michael, which still has its majestic single nave, eighty-two feet long, beneath a cradle vault twenty-six feet high, and a handsome semicircular limestone doorway. There is also a house of the Knights Templar, built in the eleventh century and then remodelled in the fifteenth, and a chapel of the Pénitents Blancs, which once contained relics of St Theodore. However, it is perhaps by walking at length around the quaint arcaded streets which wind their way up the slopes that the visitor will best capture the rough but authentic flavor of this piece of the Middle Ages.

At the confluence of the Giscle and the Môle, we now come to Cogolin, a large village which, having chosen not to make the sacrifices traditionally associated with the tourist business, has bravely struck out on its own, by concentrating on original handicrafts. These include pipes made from local briar, reeds for musical instruments, fishing rods, natural cork, and handmade carpets woven in a workshop set up in 1922 by Armenian refugees.

Grimaud. The village in its natural setting (above); the church (below); the remains of the castle (below and facing page).

Houses at Cogolin (left). View of the Dom Forest (above). Ancient pine and cork oaks in the Maures region (facing page, bottom).

The remains of a medieval bastion and windmill look down from the sloping ground above Cogolin, which was fortified in the fifteenth century by the Knights of Malta. Other interesting sights are the clock tower and the old town gate. The church of Saint-Sauveur, built in the eleventh century (1085), is of particular interest. Though enlarged in the fifteenth century, it still retains the nave and the belltower of the original structure. Inside, the visitor will be rewarded by the sight of a superb altarpiece and some fine wooden statues from the seventeenth century, as well as a triptych of 1540, signed Hurlepin. The most recent historic event associated with Cogolin occurred in August 1944, when General De Lattre de Tassigny established his headquarters there.

Beyond Cogolin we move up the Môle Valley towards Hyères. The village of La Môle is situated at the edge of the Dom Forest, and at the confluence of the Verne river, which flows from the hills around the Carthusian monastery. It is known only through the small airport which serves Saint-Tropez, whereas its ungainly but romantic eleventh cen-tury castle, which sports two pepper-pot towers, is largely ignored. Yet Saint-Exupéry had his Little Prince run across the sloping grounds of that castle, at the edge of the forest of chestnut trees. Nearby is the magnificent Dom Forest, made famous by Jean Aicart, who used it as the setting for the exploits of Maurin des Maures.

THE RAMATUELLE PENINSULA

The road which comes directly from Saint-Tropez, via La Foux and the Cogolin Marina, crosses the isthmus of the peninsula, in an undulating region of croplands and vineyards, which, though pleasant, is not particularly interesting.

The natural setting of La Croix-Valmer is different. Ringed by wooded hills, it appears to have been cast in the mould of a broad valley, descending to the sea some two miles away. During its heyday at the turn of the century it acquired some princely villas and palatial hotels, which have since been turned into apartments. Dotted about among the foliage, its villas line the long wide avenues leading to the bay, and lend the whole place a tranquil air.

The huge stone cross in the center of the village is a reminder of the legend from which the village derives its name. At this spot, in 312, a shining cross appeared to Emperor Constantine who was on his way to Gaul to defend Christianity, thus serving as a prophecy of his victory over the pagan forces.

The beaches of La Croix-Valmer stretch out along Cavalaire Bay, with

names redolent of thyme and garlic: Bouillabaisse, Sylvabelle, Gigaro. The deep shoreline which not too long ago was wild and deserted, has now, unfortunately, become more and more heavily developed. This route will enable us to discover the peninsula itself, with its coastline, its landscapes and its villages.

The windy and hilly road leads through picturesque scenery to the top of Collebasse pass, at an altitude of 425 ft. From here there is a superb view of two bays: Cavalaire and Pampelonne.

Thereafter, in a landscape of ancient grandeur strongly reminiscent of the Roman *campagna*, we come to Ramatuelle. This delightful perched village, situated unusually low at 445 ft, looks exactly like an eagle's nest. Clinging to the slopes of a wooded outcropping of rock, its houses are huddled tightly together so that, taken as a whole, they form a rampart which resembles the *Ksour* of Tunisia. In the middle of the village there is a square with a church which, at least in its present shape, dates from the seventeenth century, and a huge elm, said to be the only survivor of a group of trees planted there by Sully. All around is a maze of tangled, winding streets, narrow and steep, crossed occasionally by arches and covered passageways which impart a truly medieval atmosphere.

As we walk around them we came to realize that Ramatuelle must have had a difficult history. Occupied by the Saracens for sixty years, besieged by the members of the League during the wars of religion, it has been forced to defend itself throughout its entire history. Today the only invaders are the tourists, who are also attracted by the tomb of Gérard Philipe, who died in 1955 and lies buried in the tiny cemetery with the black cypresses.

From Ramatuelle to Gassin the road passes various country houses and estates on its way through this landscape of vineyards and forests. Colette dubbed it a "branch of paradise on earth"–this land with such radiant light, changing and pure, with lush and varied vegetation which includes both fig trees and umbrella pines, eucalyptus trees and the more common deciduous species which one tends to forget about in this part of the world. On the way we pass near three mills, the Moulins de Paillas, now in ruins. This, the highest point on the peninsula, at 1,070 ft, is a splendid vantage point formely much used by the lookouts of the village of Ramatuelle.

Gassin, another sentinel village, standing at 660 ft, at the top of a rocky escarpment which rises out of the wooded landscape below, has not lost its medieval allure. Founded in the twelfth century by the Knights Templar on the site of a Saracen citadel, it still has well-preserved ramparts, enclosing its venerable houses which, on account of the limits inherent in the village's position, are packed very close together. Its twelfth century Romanesque church, which is still attractive despite some later remodelling, contains a handsome bust of St Lawrence (sixteenth century) and a contemporary stations of the cross (1968), the work of Roger Roux.

View of Ramatuelle (facing page, top). A traditional farmhouse in the nearby vineyards (facing page, bottom).

Gassin: a street and overall view (top). Tahiti beach (above). Following pages: aerial view of Ramatuelle.

29

THE GULF OF SAINT-TROPEZ

Saint-Tropez was originally a Greek colony, Heraclia Cacarabia, so named on account of its temple of Hercules (in Greek, Herakles) which was famous for its oracles.

In 68 Tropes, a Roman soldier who was a native of Pisa, was beheaded on the orders of Nero because he had dared proclaim his Christian faith in the Emperor's presence. Strange though it may seem, his body was then placed in a boat, between a rooster and a dog, and left to its fate on the waves. With the passage of time the martyr's remains became an object of pilgrimage, so that by the fourth century, his tomb had given the town its definitive name. Eventually, after the disappearance of the ancient trading posts, Saint-Tropez, like all of the coast, fell a prey to the unceasing raids of Arab marauders.

Having been completely destroyed in 739 and then in 888 by the Saracens, it was abandoned by its inhabitants, who took refuge further inland. It was not until 1470–more than four centuries later–that Jean de Cossa, a seneschal, or chief steward, of Provence, tried to revive its fortunes. He gave the town to a Genoese lord, Raphael de Garezzio, promising the people total exemption from taxes and levies provided that they rebuilt the town and agreed to defend it. The new citizens of Saint-Tropez kept their end of the bargain so well in the sixteenth and seventeenth cen-

turies that they repelled all marauders, fortified the town, and even succeeded, on June 15 1637, right in the middle of the Thirty Years' War, in routing twenty-one Spanish galleys which were trying to land troops there.

After 1677, when it became a possession of the Suffren family, the town basked in the prestige and glory of the great mariner.

The Revolution and the Empire brought Saint-Tropez oblivion, which was not to be dispelled until the end of the nineteenth century by the arrival of the painters, who were drawn by the charm of its small harbor and the special light in which it was bathed. Paul Signac (1863-1935) settled there in 1892, anxious to capture the colors of the hinterland and the immense serenity and purity of the landscape. He also told his friends about his new-found paradise; first of all some other painters, such as Matisse, Bonnard, Marquet, Dunoyer de Segonzac, and later on ministers, writers and artists–in fact anyone who was anyone in the Paris of the day.

However, it is during the off-season that the village recovers the radiant poetic attractiveness which so fascinated the artists of the nineteenth century. Though it lacks any major architectural treasures Saint-Tropez is still a most rewarding place to visit. However, the old harbor, sheltered behind the seawall which ends in a lighthouse, has preserved its subtle charm–at least when it is not invaded by yachts so tightly packed together that they can hardly move. And the waterfront itself is most pleasant, except when submerged in an unceasing to and fro of

Saint-Tropez. The Citadel: one of the bastions (left). The harbor and the famous bay (facing page). Following pages: the waterfront.

ephemeral celebrities. The statue of the bailiff of Suffren, which is normally barely noticed amidst the throngs of vacationers in summertime, can then be seen more clearly. It certainly deserves to be noticed, because the bailiff in question was a remarkable man. Born in 1726, near Aix-en-Provence, his family residence was at Saint-Tropez, on the Place de l'Hôtel de Ville. Having shown considerable prowess in the service of the Knights of Malta, he achieved glory in the Royal French Navy at the age of 55, when, during a prodigious campaign in the Indies, he defeated an English fleet. After being promoted to the rank of King's Admiral, he died at the age of 66, from an ill-advised blood-letting. The portly, brilliant and fearless stra-

tegist was one of France's greatest seafarers.

The old town, a labyrinth of cobble-stoned streets, with rooftops of red Roman tiles, leads to La Ponche, the nicest creek in Saint-Tropez. This delightful, tiny fishing beach, which is lined by old houses in the Italian style, painted in soft faded colors, indicates the Genoese origins of the town. The inlet of La Glaye, formerly much used by fishermen, is flanked by the Daumas tower and a fort from the year 880, both built by Guillaume I, Count of Provence. They are all that remains of the feudal city.

The extremely well preserved Citadel stands proudly on its hilltop. The large central fort was built from 1583 onwards, though the fortress as

a whole, enclosed within a tall crenellated defensive wall, fortified with bastions, dates from the seventeenth century. Besides serving as a vantage point with a fine view of the town and its harbors, it is also the setting for a number of summer festivals, and houses a naval museum with a wide range of exhibits.

The seventeenth century chapel of L'Annonciade, situated on the waterfront, was turned into a museum of modern art in 1955. It combines the principal works of the painters who either lived at Saint-Tropez or were very fond of the town: Vlaminck, Derain, Braque, Seurat, Cross, Bonnard, Dufy, Rouault, Van Dongen and so many others who came here to join Signac, the man who had in a sense «invented» the resort.

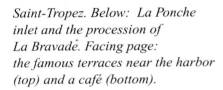

Saint-Tropez. Below: La Ponche inlet and the procession of La Bravade. Facing page: the famous terraces near the harbor (top) and a café (bottom).

Port-Grimaud (above and facing page). Following pages: overall view of the remarkable development at Port-Grimaud.

FROM SAINTE-MAXIME TO FRÉJUS

Port-Grimaud is situated beyond the Giscle Delta, which has buried the former port of Grimaud beneath the marshes.

This lakeside community is an interesting architectural experiment, on which F. Spoerry started construction in 1964. In imitation of Italian fishing villages, the houses, all of which are different, are attached to one another, and colored in gentle pastel tones. The front of each one looks out over a canal, to which a small pontoon provides access. There is also a network of streets and small squares.

The villas of Beauvallon, deep within an immense pine grove which covers its rocky slopes, are located in a truly superb setting, which must have been a haven of richly scented peace in the days when Paul Géraldy and Joseph Peyré decided to live there.

Sainte-Maxime is a luxury seaside and winter resort which receives large numbers of visitors each year. This beautiful spot was once occupied by a Phocean trading station (Calidianis), before being fortified by the monks of Lérins as a defense against pirate raids. For added protection, this time of a divine nature, they gave it the name of a saint, the legendary daughter of the Count of Grasse, feudal lord of Antibes.

Commerce brought it short-lived prosperity in the seventeenth century, when its harbor was used as a port of call by sailing vessels carrying wine, oil and timber between Marseille and Italy. However, it was not until the nineteenth century that this charming Provençal village was elevated to the rank of high-society resort. There is a large beach next to the old fishing harbor, where traffic has dwindled to insignificant levels.

Sainte-Maxime's charm is greatly enhanced by the excellent walks to be had in the vicinity and by its exceptionally mild winter climate.

As far as La Nartelle, with its developments beneath the pines, the

road, swinging around Cap des Sardineaux, runs very close to the shore, past a stretch of fine properties with magnificent gardens.

Shortly thereafter the villas become less expensive-looking, and the vegetation somewhat less abundant. Here we come to a number of more modest and relaxed resorts, which are very appealing. La Garonnette, a long strip of land between the road and the sea, has a number of small beaches with handsome cliffs, and, in the background, a superb and undeveloped hill. At Val d'Esquières the beach is tiny, but there is a splendid valley which opens into the quiet Bougnon bay. We find the same contrast again at San-Peïré: a narrow beach with a small harbor for pleasure craft, but a scenic hill. Along this part of the coast beauty tends to be concentrated inland, rather than along the sea.

That all changes, however, once we come to Issambres, whose name derives from that of the Cimbrian tribes who first settled on this site. Here the road moves away from the sea, yielding to a long oasis of pines which border a series of deeply indented inlets and creeks. Towards the hill we find a pleasant resort in the midst of terraces abundantly covered with vegetation; nearby there are two marinas and a large beach.

At this point on the coast the magnificent red rocks of the Esterel suddenly come into view. Their beauty remains very much in our minds as we move along the Gaillarde beach and cross Lauvette Point. And we are still under the influence of the Esterel's charm when we reach Saint-Aygulf, the last large beach of the Maures coast, which soon comes to an end at the far side of the Gulf of Fréjus.

This resort is named after a monk, Aygulf who, around the year 660, imposed the rule of the Benedictine order on the monastery of Saint-Honorat. Villas lie dotted around among groves of pine, oak and eucalyptus. The main beach is a delicate strip of fine sand, a mile and a half long, with rocks protruding into the sea at either end.

There is also a string of small beaches, which, though pebbly, are nonetheless charming, and also happen to be well shaded. In the midst of this pleasant setting an elegant modern chapel exhibits canvases by the painter Carolus-Duran, an official and high-society portraitist of the late nineteenth century (1837-1917).

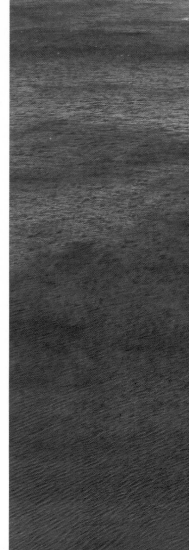

Les Issambres (top).
Saint-Aygulf (above).

The red rocks of the Esterel
(facing page).

THE HIGH VILLAGES OF THE MAURES COAST

Another route, quite as exciting as the corniche route, also leads through the Maures massif.

Situated inland from the Sainte-Maxime coast it is not very well known, but it esthetically most pleasing.

From Port-Grimaud the simplest route takes us through Saint-Pons-les-Mures, where Lucien Guitry once had a summer home, past the foot of the village of Grimaud and up the Garde Valley along a superb winding, scenic road; it runs through the forest and transports us from the enchanting world of pines and olive groves to the more majestic and wilder stands of chestnut trees.

La Garde-Freinet, clinging to the rock in the midst of the massif, at an altitude of 1,180 ft, was for many years thought to be an impregnable site.

After their defeat at the hands of Charles Martel in 732, the Arabs spread out through Upper Provence, which they found provided them with a suitable climate and reliable defensive positions. They liked the terrain at La Garde-Freinet so much that they chose it as the site for their famous fortified capital, Fraxime, at the top of the hill overlooking the present village. And it was from this base that they launched the raids which ravaged the coast from 890 to 973. They were not finally driven out of the area until Guillaume I, Count of Provence, organized a powerful campaign of conquest. In the meantime they had taught the local inhabitants the use of cork and resin, the tambourine and varnished tiles. In this and other ways the Arabs brought progress and civilization to the Western world.

Their citadel, which was destroyed in the fifteenth century, now consists of nothing more than some proud but tattered ruins, spectacularly located on high ground with panoramic views.

The village, which still derives its livelihood from its traditional handicrafts, the small-scale manufacture of cork and glazed chestnuts, consists of a host of converging red-tiled rooftops clustered around the square, stout belltower of an imposing Romanesque-Provençal church.

Here we are in the midst of one of the wildest forests of the Maures massif; the soil is poor, thin and dry, allowing only for the survival of genistas, agaves and heather. Vast expanses of sun-baked garrigue alternate with cork oaks and Aleppo pines. It is easy to understand why the Arabs must have felt very much at home here.

Turning off the roads to Vidauban and Cannet-des-Maures, which go north beyond the area which we shall be covering, we shall cut across the massif, taking some magnificent mountain roads, which wind their way through the rugged terrain, which includes some genuine Provençal scenery. The Vignon Pass (1,150 ft) takes us to Plan-de-la-Tour, a large and sleepy village situated on a high plateau whose vineyards are renowned for their rich wine and a rather surprising sparkling rosé with a raspberry flavor.

Despite its innocuous appearance, this high mountain village had always had an attraction for strange phenomena; at one time it was the domain of shameless witches who specialized in overturning carts.

Passing through the villages of Valaury and Les Pierrons, we now came to the Gratteloup Pass (740 ft), which connects with the road from Le Muy to Sainte-Maxime. Nearby is the estate of Saint-Donat, an unusual amusement park. One particularly noteworthy feature is a rare and exciting museum of mechanical music, which introduces the visitor to the wonderful world of Barbary organs and music boxes. Saint-Donat is also the point of departure for the most interesting excursion to Le Vieux Revest, an abandoned village whose moving ruins stand in perpetual slumber amidst the silence and the scents of the steep wooded valleys of the Maures Massif, huddled around their equally dead ghost church.

FRÉJUS

On its rocky plateau overlooking the alluvial plain of the Argens Delta–an oasis of vines and fruit trees–the ancient town of Fréjus is gradually moving further and further away from the sea.

The small Celto-Ligurian oppidum discovered by Caesar in 49 BC was in those days near the coast–this doubtless being what prompted him to build his Forum Julii, as a way station on the road from Italy to Gaul which was eventually to become the Aurelian Way. After the assassination of Caesar, Octavius, later the Emperor Augustus, who needed a powerful fleet, turned Forum Julii into a huge naval base, consisting of both a port and naval shipyards. The long years of the Pax Romana diminished the importance of this essentially military complex. From the eighth to the tenth centuries, Barbary pirates hastened the decline of the town, while the Saracens completed their work of devastation in 940. However, Bishop Riculphe, from 975 to 990, revived it by building the episcopal compound, which is the heart of the medieval village and the precursor of the present town.

Visitors to Fréjus come looking for reminders of its ancient and medieval grandeur. The remains of the Roman colony–the oldest buildings in Provence–are not commensurate with the splendor of its past. Having been built of small stone blocks, for the sake of speed and efficiency in construction, they are quite lacking in ornamental features and have not withstood the ravages of time as well as the civic monuments of the other great Roman cities in Gaul.

The colony of Augustus was really nothing more than a huge, military camp, built of masonry and surrounded by more than 9,185 ft of thick ramparts. The ancient port, in which Augustus took great pride, no longer exists. Similarly the gigantic aqueduct, which at 30 miles was one of the longest in the Roman Empire, is now merely a row of ruined pillars and arcades, visible for the most part as one leaves the town traveling east.

Only the ruins of the theater still conjure up visions of the ancient world, although they consist largely of the radiating masonry structure which supported the tiered seats. The arena, which was built about the same time as the theater, is situated slightly outside the city walls, at the foot of a hill. Though not the biggest of its kind in Gaul, it is certainly the oldest.

The Bishop's Palace is the other important historic building in Fréjus. This superb fortified complex is arranged in a very dense layout around Place Formigé, in the center of the present town. It was founded around the year 370, at the time of the establishment of the diocese of Fréjus. The Baptistry also dates from the late fourth century. This austere and solid square structure, with sides measuring 35 ft, contains eight recesses arranged in an octagonal pattern around the interior. The only decorative concession in its design was a white marble and mosaic floor, as well as black granite columns with capitals taken from the Roman forum. The large octagonal basin in the middle was used for baptism. The ornately door panels were added in the sixteenth century.

The present cathedral was built in the tenth century by Bishop Riculphe, over the remains of a fortified basilica from the same period as

*The ruins of the amphitheater
at Fréjus (left).
The cathedral (below).*

the Baptistry. The nave is very pure and plain. The original ceiling was replaced in the twelfth century by the vaults we see today. The carved wooden choir stalls in the Gothic style date from the fifteenth century. The adjacent cloister, however, is much more remarkable, with its graceful galleries and their slender columns, from the twelfth and thirteenth centuries, surrounding a small garden with the customary stone well. Its handsome beamed ceiling having replaced the original vaults, this structure has great charm and elegance. It also contains some most curious paintings which show clear Spanish influence, from the fourteenth and fifteenth centuries, depicting fantastic animals and grotesque figures from the Apocalypse.

Similarly the chapterhouse, which is attached to the Baptistry, has an excellent fortified façade from the thirteenth century. Jacques d'Euze, who became Pope John XXII in 1316, and Cardinal de Fleury, Louis XVI's tutor, were the most eminent bishops to serve this illustrious domain.

SAINT-RAPHAËL

An hour should be set aside for the trip to picturesque Roquebrune-sur-Argens.

It is a medieval village on the banks of the Argens, where it is protected by the towering Roquebrune cliffs. This tiny mountain range, whose altitude does not exceed 1,210 ft, slightly apart from the Maures massif, is noteworthy for the unusual contours of its bare and jagged red sandstone, deeply indented with cliffs and spectacular ravines.

Beauty and elegance have long been associated with Saint-Raphaël. Picasso lived there in 1919. Pougny lived and painted there from 1933 to 1935. This famous resort attracts visitors both in winter, with its mild climate, and also in summer, on account of its sheltered beaches and its harbor for pleasure craft. Although it was the twin sister of Fréjus and, like it, a daughter of Rome, its destiny followed a very different path. Its remarkable location, near the first foothills of the Esterel range, first attracted the Ligurians and then all the seafarers of ancient times–mainly of course, the Romans, who settled there and at Fréjus at the same time.

However, instead of being a utilitarian city like Fréjus, Saint-Raphaël was from the start a Gallo-Roman resort built in terraces on the site of today's Grand Casino. With its lavish villas, decorated with mosaics, its sophisticated thermal baths and an astonishing vivarium, it was already a luxury resort for vacationing Roman dignitaries.

After being laid waste by the customary pirate raids, Saint-Raphaël

Two views of Saint-Raphaël from the harbor.

first became a possession of the monks of Lérins, who in 1040 rebuilt a first village around the church, called San Rafeu, which was fortified and defended by the Knights Templar in the twelfth and thirteenth centuries. The small fishing port, with 650 inhabitants, which in the turmoil of the Revolution had been renamed Barraston in honor of Barras, was really put on the map by Bonaparte's landing there in 1799, on his way back from Egypt.

It so happens that he returned, a defeated man, to embark from Saint-Raphaël for the island of Elba on 28 April 1814. Alphonse Karr, the controversial journalist and pamphleteer, fleeing the Paris of the Second Empire, took refuge there in 1864 and stayed until his death in 1890 in his famous Maison Close, at 313 Avenue Poincaré. Overwhelmed by the mildness of the climate and lushness of the vegetation, he urged his friends to move to the resort, whose reputation was steadily growing. He used to tell them, admiringly, that if they planted a cane in his garden they would find roses growing on it next morning.

Berlioz, Gounod and Lamartine also came and were suitably impressed. In 1867 Gounod wrote his *Romeo and Juliet* at his villa L'Oustalet dou Capelan, on the Avenue du Touring-Club. Between 1878 and 1880 the mayor of Saint-Raphaël,

Félix Martin, completed the conversion of the port into a fashionable resort, whose first loyal patrons were Gallieni, Prince Albert (the future king of Belgium) and Jean Aicard. The elegant and refined spa, which has all the necessary amenities, including a golf course, a casino and yacht club, is clearly far more impressive than any of the local ancient architecture which might claim the attention of the vacationer.

However, in the old town one should really see the handsome church of the Templars, the Provençal-Romanesque structure which was fortified in the twelfth century, serving as a place of refuge for the villagers during pirate raids.

View of the red rocks of the Esterel coast (above). Views of Agay (top, right) and Anthéor (bottom, right).

THE ESTEREL COAST

Between Saint-Raphaël and La Napoule the Esterel mountains are the star attraction.

Separated from the Maures massif by the Argens Valley, here we are in very different terrain indeed. In fact the Esterel is a huge citadel of jagged, eruptive rocks carved by erosion.

Despite its modest altitude (2,027 ft at the highest point) it conveys the impression of being a real mountain, since it is bare and rugged, with narrow ravines and short jagged ridges, and its contours remain equally contorted all the way down to the sea, where it forms a series of inlets and creeks, often quite small, wedged between sheer rock faces.

Wherever one looks, the strangeness of the shapes is heightened by the fantasy of their coloring. Here the porphyries, which are predominantly red, with a range of flamboyant tones, are sometimes blue, like those much sought after by the Romans for the columns of their buildings. The slopes are covered with the dense vegetation consisting of heather, lavender, genista and arbutus, like a tousled shock of hair which bursts into a thousand colors at blossom time. The name Golden

Corniche which is often given to the Esterel coast, really fails to match one's visual impression of it. For eighteen miles, the Esterel consists of a dazzling, chaotic mixture of red rocks plunging into a blue sea. The name Ruby Coast, which is occasionally associated with it, better conveys its main coloring.

After Aigue-Bonne Bay we come to Le Dramont, a tiny resort at the foot of a rugged headland, which has been turned into a park, and which has been bypassed by the highway. On the narrow but beautiful beach we find ourselves in the midst of bright red porphyry, with subtle green and blue outcroppings here and there.

It would be hard to imagine a more splendid setting for a summer and winter seaside resort than that of the town of Agay, which is situated at the edge of a deep roadstead, the best along the coast, in fact, being protected from all the winds. Here nature has conspired to blur seasonal differences. From the Ligurians to the Romans, all of the merchants, soldiers and pirates of the Mediterranean world, one after another, eagerly occu-

Le Trayas Bay (left). Some villas along the coast (right). The marina at Port-la-Galère (below).

pied this exceptional place. A rocky bastion of red porphyry, the Rastel d'Agay towers from an altitude of 945 ft over the resort and the coast. On 21 July 1944 Saint-Exupéry flew over his family château at Agay, where his sister lived, shortly before being reported missing out to sea.

From Agay to Anthéor, the road runs along the rather heavily developed coastline, which is nonetheless wooded and has some very attractive small inlets of red porphyry. On each shore a new picture-postcard scene comes into view, consisting of the bright red of the rocks, sprinkled with patches of green pine and bathed in the intense blue of the sea, which is strewn with a host of small islands, the largest of which is Les Vieilles.

The most scenic part of this route, however, lies between Anthéor and Le Trayas. For some four miles, we here see the Esterel in all its glory: its turbulent terrain bristling with

ridges, and slashed by ravines, advances into the sea as tongues of jagged rock, crumbling into a myriad islets. Its rocky claws embrace many tiny sunbaked bays or equally tiny beaches of rust-colored pebbles, nestling inside inlets which are sometimes very hard to reach.

Le Trayas, whose name curiously derives from the word for cable, is a charming little town, which straddles both sea and mountain. Its lower reaches are festooned with a spectacular series of inlets, enclosing some superb minuscule beaches, wedged in between the ubiquitous red rocks, or bristling here and there with green tufts of pine.

The largest of the beaches at Le Trayas lies in the inlet known as La Figueirette, which in the seventeenth century was a major tuna fishing center. For four months at a time it was blocked off by a series of fixed nets, awaiting the shoals of fish,

whose arrival was promptly signalled by lookouts stationed in the tower situated on high ground.

Miramar literally means "look at the sea"–hardly a necessary command, as the elegant and high-class resort of that name, which is also built partly on the shore and partly on rocky slopes, is singularly well set, in a frame of red rocks, strewn with small groves of mimosa.

The highway, situated as on a balcony 263 ft above the sea, is all the more spectacular in that it remains fairly undeveloped. Here the Esterel ends in twisted red cliffs, forming creeks with sheer rock walls, to which access can be very difficult.

On the promontory which forms the west end of La Napoule, the small resort of La Galère sits clinging to the slopes of the Esterel. Port-la-Galère, situated nearby at the edge of a jagged headland, is an ultramodern marina, built in the Provençal style.

THE GULF OF LA NAPOULE

We have passed the stupendous vantage points overlooking twisted inlets, ravines covered with undergrowth, and glistening rock faces which, from Miramar to La Galère, are the sad farewell of the fading Esterel range.

View of Théoule, with Cannes Bay in the background (above). La Napoule Castle (facing page).

We are suddenly treated to a new and splendid revelation: the sweeping curve of Cannes Bay, whose violet horizon is festooned with the snowy white peaks of the Alps of Upper Provence.

We have now left the solitary and practically deserted world of the Esterel Corniche, made to delight the eyes and the fantasies of the traveler, but not for living, where the water in each creek seems to be a different color and where each promontory its own shade of porphyry, and entered a landscape of tranquil and spacious harmony. The rugged has become smooth, and the jarring stimulus of colors is now the languid elegance of subtle shading.

The sea front at Théoule consists of a number of small and well-sheltered sand and pebble beaches which lie within that rare phenomenon, a beach facing north. The resort itself is situated in a valley at right angles

to the coast, which cuts through the last of the Esterel foothills.

La Napoule marks the end of the mountain and the beginning of the Cannes plain. This most pleasant resort town is famous for its enormous beach, which runs for over four miles along the edge of the gulf as far as La Croisette, which is merely its continuation. The view is still majestic, but the Esterel is no more to be seen.

The town of La Napoule itself lies huddled at the foot of the San Peyré promontory, huddled around its fourteenth century castle, which the American sculptor Henry Clews restored in 1919 in order to house his works. After his death in 1937 it became a permanent art exhibit. With its unmistakably new towers and fortifications, at the water's edge, the ivy-covered castle looks more like an operatic stage-set than a feudal fortress.

Behind the main beach lies the town of Mandelieu, whose well-to-do neighborhoods reach as far as the outskirts of Cannes, along the Siagne. The name means «place of command», and dates from the period when Mandelieu was an ancient trading post. On the Vignerons estate, situated on the most easterly slopes of the Esterel, an abbey of monks from Lérins was built on the site of a third century temple to Mithra. Excavations have been conducted at a large Gallo-Roman villa located nearby.

To the east of the town the hillock named after Saint Cassien, which was settled in ancient times, was the site of the village of Arluc, situated on the great Via Julia-Augusta linking Italy to Fréjus. Mimosa is cultivated extensively in the vicinity of Mandelieu, where the fields are scented and golden every spring.

THE ESTÉREL MASSIF

The path of National Route 7 was the same as that of the Aurelian Way, one of the most important roads in the Roman Empire.

The strip of paved and cambered roadway, slightly more than 8 ft wide, followed a tortuous route around the edge of the massif, which in ancient times posed an insurmountable obstacle.

In 1740 President De Brosses, a magistrate and writer who was also a keen archeologist, found it "the most beautiful road in the world". However, it was also one of the most dangerous, as the mountains provided a haven for all sorts of bandits, who used to stop travelers and relieve them of their possessions. There was such insecurity along the steep and deserted upland roads that the expression "crossing the Esterel" came to be synonymous with danger and prowess.

Our discovery of this region begins at La Napoule. The main road to Fréjus, the famous Route Nationale 7, is pleasant and fast, despite the volume of traffic. Its great beauty derives from its exceptional environment, which is typical of the roads which cross the Maures Massif through the Dom Forest. The astonishing thing about this route is that there are no villages along the way. From La Napoule to Fréjus there are no built-up areas, not even a hamlet. For seventeen and a half miles the traveler is alone with the mountains, the undergrowth and the sun.

The terrain is rugged and the valleys are deep, with here and there a sheer ravine or a jagged peak.

All that now remains of the original forests, which have been decimated by fires, is a few still majestic stands of trees. Crooked pines and cork oaks wrapped with leather after the harvest compete with lentisks, genistas and lavender for the honor of carpeting the mountainside.

Along the way the only trace of human habitation is to be found off the national highway, in the form of two tiny hamlets: Seguret-l'Eglise and, more particularly, Les Adrets-de-l'Esterel.

At an altitude of 843 ft, in a superb location, its few houses are clustered near the famous inn, the Auberge des Adrets. Rebuilt in 1653 and restored in 1898, it was used for a while as the base of operations for Gaspard de Besse, a famous outlaw and sort of local mandarin, who for several years robbed merchants and travelers in the Esterel. After his arrest at the age of twenty-five, in 1781, he was drawn alive and his head was nailed to a tree on the road which had been the scene of his crimes.

Until the end of the nineteenth century the whole of this wild, uninhabited region, where travel was so difficult, continued to be home to escaped convicts from the penitentiary at Toulon. The forest house at Malpey, which means "bad mountain", perpetuates the memory of that period of insecurity and high drama.

In comparison Valescure has the air of an aristocratic annex to Saint-Raphaël, with its vast and sumptuous park of magnificent umbrella pines, interspersed with luxurious villas and hotels.

The Estérel Corniche and the expressway.

CANNES

This prestigious city, on the shores of the Gulf of La Napoule, facing the Lérins Islands, is famous the world over.

Not only for the beauty of its natural setting and its blissful climate but also for the magnificence of its festivals, Cannes has been pampered by nature, which has given it fine sand, fresh water springs, sunshine, miraculous vegetation and a calm sea, in the words of Théodore de Banville. Add to that its effortless elegance and class, and one realizes why it is so popular as a summer resort besides being the winter resort of the world's aristocracy.

Looking at this magnificent city, sheltered from the winds by a majestic amphitheater of scented hills and bordered by a brilliant fringe of fair sand, who could ever visualize the small trading post of the Oxybians, a Ligurian tribe, the first settlers on the site, in the second century BC? By the name of Aegitna it was in those days merely a convenient shallow beach, surrounded by marshes, on which boats could be pulled ashore. However, the Greeks of Antipolis, the modern Antibes, annoyed by the unruly behavior of their Ligurian neighbors, arranged for the Romans to expel them in 154 BC, and replace them with other Greeks, from Marseille. Settled on the ruins of Le Suquet, they built the Castrum Marcellinum, which was a prosperous port of call for several centuries.

In the tenth century Guillaume Gruetta, son of the Count of Antibes, ceded the small medieval port of Canoïs to the monks of Lérins Island. They promptly proceeded to fortify the village and the

hill overlooking the port. They kept a watch for suspect vessels and defense was provided by the military orders, initially the Knights Templar, and then the Knights of Malta. While the Fathers of Mercy ransomed the Christians taken prisoner by the Saracens.

Although totally tax-free from 1131 onwards, the village still experienced difficulties for several centuries; being on the invasion route it became a prey for the Spanish, Austrian and Savoyard armies which successively ravaged it from 1524 to 1635. To make matters worse, severe outbreaks of the plague between 1347 and 1580 completed the havoc wrought by military disasters.

In 1788, however, with the lifting of the tutelage of the monks of Lérins, Cannes became independent. At the time it was merely a small marshy harbor besieged by the reeds (cannae) from which it derives its name.

Napoleon's landing at Golfe-Juan, on his return from Elba on 1 March 1815, began to dispel the oblivion in which it lived. Preceded by Cambronne, the Emperor requested several thousand rations in order to put out false rumors as to the size of his force, and he camped outside the town, among the dunes which then surrounded the chapel of Notre-Dame-du-Bon-Voyage, before marching on Grasse.

The resort we know today was really launched as a result of an incident, in 1834, when a British chancellor, Lord Brougham, on his way to Nice, was stopped at the passage across the Var by a *cordon sanitaire*, which had been imposed on account of an epidemic of cholera. Being thus forced to retrace his steps, and finding no way out at either Fréjus and La Napoule, he was obliged to move temporarily into the way station at Cannes. Thereafter the charm

Cannes. Suquet Hill (above, left).
The old harbor (above, right).

of the place worked quickly. Fascinated by such a pleasant natural setting he decided to have a mansion built for himself at the foot of Les Gardes Hill; this was the Eleonore-Louise Château.

Every winter for thirty-four years, until his death in 1868, he returned faithfully, gradually bringing with him the whole of the English aristocracy.

Cannes thereafter became the Queen of the Côte d'Azur. Its rise to prominence was aided, of course, by the building of the railroad and then the highway (1903).

Luxury hotels were constructed, and La Croisette and the marine gardens were laid out at the end of the Second Empire. Festivities were even devised in order ta attract and retain visitors: international regattas; the film festival, since 1946; "Midem" for the past few years; and festivals of flowers, especially the mimosa, which was imported in 1835 from the Dominican Republic and now covers some two thousand acres. Thousands of tons of mimosa flowers are exported all over Europe every year. Between 1884 and 1888 Maupassant visited Cannes on his yacht, the *Bel Ami*, long before Churchill; in his bock *On the water*, he described the enthusiasm which the town aroused in him. Mérimée went to Cannes to die in 1870 and Gérard Philipe was born there in 1922.

It is the modern city of Cannes, and most particularly its legendary Croisette, that attracts visitors. This extraordinary boulevard, lined with splendid palm trees, grand hotels and luxury apartment buildings throughout its one and a half miles, looks down over the kind of beach that dreams are made of. This is the place to meet stars, artists and in general famous people, whether they are painters or politicians, athletes or writers.

Starting at the Renaldo-Hahn Gardens, after the municipal casino and opposite the church of Notre-Dame-du-Bon-Voyage, on the site where Napoleon camped out on the night of 1 March 1815, it ends at the Palm Beach peninsula, site of one of the most celebrated casinos on the Côte d'Azur, which was built in 1929.

For souvenir-hunters the old town, which has a special cachet of its own, is also interesting. Nothing is left of the old port of Cannois, which has been replaced by a modern port, where one can see a veritable forest of masts, and even some ships. The Albert-Edouard jetty, built in 1904 in honor of the Prince of Wales, a faithful devotee of Cannes, was where Alain Gerbault set sail on 23 April 1925 for his solo voyage around the world. Behind it, the steep Suquet Hill provides the last reminder of the old quarters, which lie clustered on the slopes of Mount Chevalier. At the top, on Place de la Castre, where a few sections of fortified wall still stand, there are two buildings from the medieval past of Cannes. The church of Notre-Dame-de-L'Espérance, built between 1521 and 1648 in the Provençal Gothic style, has only a few polychrome gilded wood statues of the fifteenth and sixteenth centuries; while the Suquet Tower, a square structure built in 1070, at the time of Abbot Aldebert, which formerly served as a watchtower, retains some dilapidated fortifications and a circular bastion.

That same enchantment attracted a number of artists, and more particularly painters, who were uniquely sensitive to the magical lure of the place and its light. Puvis de Chavanne, Carolus Duran and Van Dongen were regular visitors to Cannes.

Vuillard, as well as Meissonier and Pougny, stayed here; and the Dane Williamsen died here in 1958. J.-G. Doumergue came to depict the exciting years of the high-living Belle Epoque of Cannes, from 1920 to 1930. His lavishly ornate villa, in the Florentine style, named Fiesole, which he had built in a large park bright with flower blossom, has now been turned into a museum.

Not even the greatest names of all could stay away: Renoir painted from 1901 to 1904 in a villa of Le Cannet. In 1925 Bonnard bought the property of Le Bosquet, where he settled permanently in 1947; and in 1954 Picasso bought an enormous nineteenth century country house in the hills, La Californie, where he painted in a Baroque studio until he moved to Mougins.

Cannes. La Croisette (facing page, bottom). Hôtel Carlton (left). View of the gardens of the Villa Domergue (right). The bay at sunset (below).

THE LÉRINS ISLANDS

Lying at anchor a few hundred yards off La Croisette, for which they provide a tranquil marine background, these two islands are easy to reach and very pleasant to visit.

Lacking in fresh water, yet kept lush by the humidity of the surrounding sea, they at various times attracted all the rulers of the Mediterranean, none of whom remained in control of them for very long. After a brief episode of Ligurian occupation, during which sacrifices were offered to a mysterious deity named Lero, the Romans set up a trading port of call for their fleets. They were, however, unable to retain their grip on the islands for long, and by the fourth century the islands were once again deserted. In 375, Saint Honorat, a hermit from Cape Roux who was being made increasingly uncomfortable by the large number of disciples who came to visit his cave, drawn by his legendary wisdom and holiness, settled on the island which was later to bear his name. There he founded a monastery, while his sister Marguerite founded a convent on the neighboring island.

Sainte-Marguerite Island, which is the property of the State, covers a total of 500 acres (3,600 by 1,040 yards),

and lies just over half a mile offshore from Cannes. Like the rest of the Provençal coastline it was coveted by pirates from many different countries.

Eventually Richelieu occupied it and built its fortifications. The famous Sainte-Marguerite Fort (1685), which was built on the site of a Roman citadel, would soon be turned into a State prison. This royal fort, which was enlarged by the Spaniards and then remodeled by Vauban, is the island's main attraction, mainly because of its most illustrious inmate, the Man in the Iron Mask. Visitors are still shown the dark, damp cell where that mysterious prisoner was confined from 1687 to 1698, before being transferred to the Bastille, where he died in 1703. They are also shown the dungeon from which Marshal Bazaine escaped in 1873. According to tradition he is thought to be slipped through the skylight; however, it is much more likely, on account of his obesity, that he walked out the door in disguise, having first bribed his guards.

The rest of the island is covered with eucalyptus and umbrella pines, where crickets chirp against an azure background.

Saint Honorat Island, which is smaller, more remote and, above all, a more solitary place, is still a haven of peace and serenity, wild and unspoilt.

The Lerina of ancient times was infested with snakes when the saintly hermit arrived there for the first time. Legend has it that God killed off the reptiles and then swept their bodies into the sea, thus causing it to rise, washing over the island, while the

saint took refuge up a tree. The first monastery, which drew large numbers of disciples, was built around 410; in the sixth century it became the most famous monastery of the Christian world. Saint Aygulf introduced the Benedictine rule there around 660. However, some seventy years later, the cloister and the buildings were destroyed by the Saracens, who slaughtered the monks.

In 1070 Abbot Aldebert built a fortified monastery. Yet the looting continued for several centuries, with pirates and regular armies taking it in turns over the years to carry on the destruction. In 1859 the Bishop of Fréjus bought the island and the Abbot of Sénanque established a Cistercian community there in 1870.

Nowadays a few monks still remain on the island, cultivating the vines and distilling their traditional liqueur, which is called Lerina. All that remains of the original monastery buildings is part of the cloister and the chapter house, which date from 660 and 1073 respectively. Restoration work was ordered and carried out by Prosper Mérimée, who was at the time an inspector of national monuments.

As for the old castle on the shore, a few yards from the monastery, with its dilapidated walls standing among the pines, this was part of the fortress built in the eleventh century by Abbot Aldebert. It is actually a citadel-cum-monastery, based on the same principle as the fortified *ribats* of Morocco, in which defense and faith, military engineering and contemplation, were inseparably associated to secure the survival of the faith.

Far left: Sainte-Marguerite, the entrance of the fort.
Left: the cloisters of Saint-Honorat.
Above: the citadel monastery.

NEAR CANNES

Le Cannet, situated very near Cannes, is more than a suburb.

The harbor of Golfe-Juan (above). Picasso's famous Man with Sheep, on the square in Vallauris (facing page).

Formed by the union of fourteen outlying villages, it has become an extension of the great city itself. It has the advantage of being remarkably quiet, being set aside from the bustle of the coast. Rachel died there in 1858, and Bonnard painted there during his final years (1939-1947).

The old town, clustered around the most appropriately named Place Belle-Vue, from which there is in fact a fine view, still has a number of imposing medieval ramparts. Its two feudal towers, Calvis and Danys, of the twelfth and fifteenth centuries respectively, are remarkable for their machicolations.

As we leave Cannes the space between the hills widens appreciably, making room for Golfe-Juan.

This excellent natural harbor, chosen by Napoleon on 1 March 1815 for his return from the island of Elba, was in those days quite deserted, with nothing more than a few humble fishermen's cottages. The famous proclamation "The eagle shall fly from belltower to belltower, until it reaches the towers of Notre-Dame" was posted here, thus marking the beginning of the Route Napoléon.

Although adjacent to Golfe-Juan, the resort of Juan-les-Pins belongs to the community of Antibes. Its expansion has been due to the quality of its beach, which has excellent amenities, and to the beauty of its seafront. There is also a superb view of the Esterel. The resort, which came into being after the construction of the railroad station in 1882, was launched by the Duke of Albany, one of the sons of Queen Victoria, who even found a name for it, and most especially by the American millionaire Frank Jay Gould, who provided the dollars and the guests needed for its burgeoning growth.

The village of Vallauris, which is world-famous for its artistic pottery, lies in an amphitheater of hills covered with vineyards, as well as olive and orange trees. In its bucolic and lush setting it was the successor to a Roman farming community, Vallis Aurea, the Golden Valley, situated on the seven and a half acre Encourdoules plateau, near the chapel of Saint-Bernard.

The first Vallauris was a Gallo-Roman trading station, which then came under the control of the monks of Lérins, who took over all the thirteenth century. The «protective» monks built a fortified priory, known to them as a castle, which Turennes destroyed in 1568, leaving only the chapel standing.

As it is today the village has lost much of its medieval character. In fact the remains of the Lérins Priory, on Place de la Liberté, now attract much attention. Built in 1227, then rebuilt in the sixteenth century, in the midst of the Renaissance, it now has one sole reminder of its heyday–the Romanesque chapel, on the walls of which Picasso painted a huge fresco entitled *War and Peace*, covering a total of 1,345 square feet. It depicts the chariot of war, drawn by the horses of death, halted by a shield with a dove being brandished by the people.

Vallauris was already an important center for the manufacture of bricks and pottery in the times of Tiberius. Local resources account for this specialization: a rich seam of refractory clay, and nearby pine forests, which provided plenty of fuel for baking.

Originally production, which was of a purely utilitarian and culinary nature, was under the control of the monks of Lérins, who used to levy duties on profits. With the passage of time the output of this widely renowned pottery became artistic ceramics.

During his stay at Vallauris from 1952 to 1959, Picasso revived this ancient craft, which had fallen into a slump. His works are on display at the museum of ceramics, housed in the restored halls of the monks «castle».

Cap d'Antibes. The famous Eden-Roc villa-hotel and two views of its grounds (left and below). Overall view of the cape (above). La Garoupe park (facing page, bottom).

CAP D'ANTIBES

The Cap d'Antibes road may be tortuous, but it is an incomparably beautiful way to reach the fortified town.

In fact it does not really go all the way around the peninsula. Instead, it skirts some large tracts of land occupied by palatial mansions and gardens straight out of the *Thousand and One Nights*, situated on the coastal fringe, coyly hiding their opulence behind a discreet screen of trees, apart from the rest of the world.

The road runs along a number of developed coves–Mouton harbor, Piton moorings and Olivette harbor–before reaching the Grillon, a fortified watchtower built in the seventeenth century. It now serves as a small museum of Napoleonic memorabilia. Nearby is the Chênes Verts villa, where Jules Verne stayed and the world-famous Eden-Roc restaurant, with its beach, to which a variety of celebrities are regular visitors.

Beyond Ilette Point there is only a lighthouse, which towers over the cove known as Faux-Argent.

There are plenty of spacious paths which wind their way through the foliage of pines and mimosas, past some famous places: the Eden-Roc villa, La Croë Château, palatial estates submerged in vegetation befitting a paradise on earth, whose enchanting beauty can be only dimly discerned by the passer-by.

La Garoupe, on Cap d'Antibes.
The chapel of Notre-Dame-
du-Bon-Port (left).
The lighthouse (below) and
the park (facing page, bottom).
The small nearby harbor
of L'Olivette (facing page, top).

In such surroundings the church of Saint-Benoît serves merely as a landmark showing the way to the Boulevard de La Garoupe, which leads to the beach of the same name and to Jonquet cove, which lies in a sheltered spot behind Bacon Point.

This route takes us around La Garoupe Hill, with its lighthouse and signal-station; visitors will also find a viewing table and a handsome,

unusual chapel, Notre-Dame-du-Bon-Port.

Founded in the fifth century by the ubiquitous monks of Lérins, it was the successor to a pagan sanctuary dedicated to Selena, the moon-goddess. The good friars turned it into a primitive oratory in honor of St Helena. The similarity between the two names, Selena and Helena, was no mere coincidence; indeed such

Christian «takeovers» of pagan names were a frequent occurrence at the time. The church consists of two adjoining naves, one of the thirteenth century, and the other of the fourteenth. The altarpiece is flanked by two masterpieces which one would hardly expect to find here: a fourteenth century Russo-Byzantine icon and a marvellous piece of painted silk from the Middle Ages. Both

were originally from Sebastopol. In 1952-53, seeking to offset the eastern influence of these works, which are of course quite admirable, J.-H. Clergues painted a large historico-religious fresco on another section of the chapel wall. The substantial collection of maritime votive offerings which covers the remainder of the wall is far more moving and more human.

Each year, in July, the fishermen of Antibes come to pick up the painted wooden figure of their protectress, the Virgin Mary, and take it in a procession around the streets of Antibes.

In the middle of the peninsula Château Thénard is where Grand-Duke Nikolai of Russia died, in exile, in 1924; Villa Thuret is surrounded by a remarkable exotic garden founded in 1856 by the scientist after whom the villa is named, in order to acclimatize plants imported from warm countries.

ANTIBES

Antibes enjoys a most remarkable location, on a rocky headland facing Nice and the bay.

Antibes was formed by military necessity. The early trading stations on this site were first Etruscan, and later Ligurian (by the name of Antion); in 330 BC it became a Phocean colony, facing the city across the way–whence its name, Antipolis. Trade with the turbulent Ligurians was so fraught with uncertainty and insecurity that the inhabitants appealed to Rome for help in punishing their unruly neighbors.

In 154 BC their wishes were fulfilled, and order was restored. In 42, the increasingly prosperous city surrounded itself with defensive walls and shook off Marseille's oppressive yoke. Like Fréjus at about the same time, Antibes was then a powerful Roman city, with its own arsenal.

The barbaric invasions ruined the Roman colony and by the fifth century the city, which in the meantime had become Christian, was elevated to the status of a bishopric. It remained so until 1244, when it was transferred to Grasse. However, as the Bishop of

Grasse had carelessly chosen to side with the Roman Pope during the schism, Clement VII confiscated his property and awarded Antibes to the Grimaldi family. Throughout the Middle Ages the city was repeatedly laid waste by pirates, corsairs and the armies of Charles V or those of Savoy. When it had been restored to the French crown, it was fortified first by Henri II and then by Henri IV.

The old town, a curious coastal fringe, is still confined within its walls and reaches as far as the Cours Masséna, which exactly follows the path of the outer defensive walls of Roman times. The church, which was founded in the twelfth century, is situated in the center. Renovation in the fourteenth century meant that the only parts of the original structure to survive are the apse, the Romanesque transept and the square tower, standing separately from the sanctuary, which serves as its belltower. In the interior, the nave and all the ornamentation are from the sixteenth and seventeenth centuries.

The other leading attraction in the old town is the castle, built on a terrace overlooking the sea. Formerly a Roman castrum, it was the residence of the bishops from the fifth to the thirteenth centuries, before becoming the castle of the Grimaldi family from 1385 to 1608.

The present buildings, which were restored in 1830, are clustered around a square centrally located keep, which was built in the fourteenth century, and restored in the fifteenth. The citadel now houses an interesting Grimaldi Museum, whose main distinction is the whole floor devoted to works of Picasso from 1946.

The Promenade Amiral-de-Grasse provides a suitable conclusion to a visit to this part of Antibes. Facing out to sea, the sixteenth century ramparts, whose construction was started by Henri II in 1550, continued by Henri IV and completed by Vauban, are still intact, and rise straight out of the sea. To the west they culminate in the Saint-André bastion, an archeological museum which contains an interesting collection of shipwrecks, amphoras and underwater finds –especially the remarkable sternpost of an Etruscan vessel from the fifth century BC. At its eastern end we

come to the harbor which was built in the seventeenth century, and adapted for pleasure craft in 1970. To the east it is protected by the massive Fort Carré (Square Fort), which, despite its name, is a perfect star-shaped structure designed by Vauban in the seventeenth century, built over an original fort erected by Henri II and enlarged by Henri IV, of which one can still see the squat central tower (1150).

Outside these ramparts there is another old town, the one whose narrow streets and small squares are located around the Place Nationale. Just as the military structures to which we have just referred remind us of a tiny Monaco without a prince, so this old quarter, a favorite of Sydney Bechet, brings to mind the old Nice.

Behind the Vauban fort a colorful and picturesque flower market is held. It reminds us that the region's livelihood depends to a large extent on the cultivation of flowers. Carnations, tulips, gladioli and particularly roses, of which Antibes is the capital of Europe, are grown in 100,000 frames, on a total of 625 acres.

In such an endearing and noble setting, the august historical surroundings and the intoxicating scent of flowers attracted numerous artists: Harpignies and Monet at the end of the last century, Léger in 1934 and then Pougny, who took refuge there in 1940. Picasso returned to Antibes in 1946 to paint, in a single season, the incredible mass of varied works, ranging from ceramics to tapestry and from drawing to painting, which comprise the bulk of the collections of the Grimaldi Museum. On 15 March 1955 Nicolas de Stael committed suicide by leaping from his studio, which faced out to sea.

The tower of Antibes castle (top). View of the old town and its natural setting (facing page). Following pages: aerial view of the old town, around the castle and the cathedral, situated within the defensive walls.

FROM ANTIBES TO VILLENEUVE-LOUBET

Past Antibes the coast becomes straight, flat and less interesting, although we have already reached the splendid Baie des Anges.

The first marine zoo in Europe is located at La Brague. Its main attraction is an American-style show involving trained dolphins, in a pool 124 ft in diameter.

Vaugrenier lagoon, a short distance further on, is all that remains of the port of the ancient Oxybian Ligurians. In 154 BC this was the site of the first clash between the inhabitants of these coasts and the Roman legions which had been summoned to Gaul to help the Greek settlers in the trading stations.

The flat beach of Villeneuve-Loubet, which is exceptionally far from the village of the same name, over a mile away on the Grasse road, is merely a reference point along this harmonious yet monotonous coast, crossing the mouth of the Loup. Near the mouth of the river we come to a most interesting modern development, the Baie des Anges marina, consisting of a residential complex designed by André Minangoy around a harbor for

pleasure boats. Businesses and shops are situated on the waterfront, while an astounding cascade of terraces adorned with hanging gardens descends from the top of the apartment buildings down to the sea. This curious accumulation of quasi-ziggurats in the Babylonian style adjoining a promontory is not without dignity and originality. Next we pass the Côte d'Azur hippodrome, in the adjacent suburb of Cros-de-Cagnes, another seaside resort belonging to a village in the hinterland.

In actual fact, along this part of the Riviera the seafront tends to be less interesting and attractive than the immediate hinterland.

Biot, on the Grasse road, is in itself a very interesting village. Its houses cling to a hillside above the Brague Valley. It was here that the legendary King René, in 1470, founded a community of fifty Genoese families which he placed under the protection of the hospitalier orders, in an attempt to revive the region. Having become famous and prosperous through its pottery, which was originally utilitarian in nature, Biot continued in the same vein and has now become a major center for ceramics and artistic handicrafts. Glass artwork, the most recent such industry in the area, having been established in the fifties, has prolonged a centuries-old tradition. Visitors can now see glass being blown by means of ancient techniques.

Being aerated and illuminated by thousands of capricious bubbles which catch the light in many different ways, glass paste–a mixture of

sand, limestone and sodium carbonate melted at extremely high temperatures–is colored with oxides of manganese (violet), peat (yellow) or cobalt (blue).

In the eighteenth century the glassworks were located in the midst of pine forests, where fuel was plentiful. After 1850, however, industrial production forced the closing of the last establishment producing handmade glass.

With its sloping streets and vaulted passageways, here we find all the charm of the old villages of Provence. Just outside Biot, in the tiny village of Saint-Pierre one should be sure to take the secondary road which leads to the Mas Saint-André. This farmhouse used to be the property of Fernand Léger. The museum which was built here in 1959, after his death, was turned over to the State in 1967 by Nadia Léger. The importance and the dimensions of the works exhibited made it necessary to construct a building specially designed for the purpose; it was designed by André Svetchine.

GRASSE

Grasse is superbly located, at the top of a series of limestone terraces which form the natural amphitheater surrounding the hinterland of Cannes.

At the foot of the Roquevignon Plateau, which looks down over the long undulating plains, it is a typical small Provençal town, with lots of charm, surrounded by greenhouses and fields of flowers, where jasmine, reseda and violets vie with the traditional terraces of olive, orange and mimosa.

The precise origins of the town are unknown. Some people believe it was founded by Crassus, who gave it its name. Others feel that it traces its origins to a Jewish community which had taken refuge there after leaving Sardinia.

Queen Victoria was later to stay. To preserve her peace and quiet the bells were no longer rung and cattle no longer wore bells. Her brother Napoleon passed along that same boulevard in 1815, on his return from the island of Elba, at the start of his triumphant march on Paris.

Grasse really consists of a mixture of two towns; one is spacious and modern, with terraces and gardens at vantage points overlooking the plain, while the other is old, having changed little since the seventeenth century. Its tall, narrow Provençal houses—some of which have four or even five sto-

The rest of the old town is located on various parts of the hilltop, centering on picturesque little squares such as Place des Aires, which is surrounded by eighteenth century arcaded houses; here a delightful market is held, around a fountain with superimposed basins, in the typical Provençal style.

As we wander through the old streets we come across some interesting buildings, such as the fourteenth century oratory chapel or the Hôtel Font-Michel. There is a remarkable museum of Provençal art and history in the town house once inhabited, in the eighteenth century, by Louise de Mirabeau, the sister of the famous statesman and orator of the Revolution. It includes some very complete collections of furniture and everyday objects. Lastly, the Fragonard Museum is housed in the villas of the artist's friend Maubert, where he took refuge during the Revolution.

Besides Fragonard (1731-1806), the son of a glover-tanner, the town's other favorite son is Admiral de Grasse, who achieved immortality in the American War of Independence.

Before leaving Grasse one should visit one of its perfumeries. The whole of the Côte d'Azur, from Hyères to Menton, has perfect climatic conditions for the cultivation of flowers, but Grasse is definitely its capital city. Flowers dominate the landscape, all over the terraces which succeed one another from the rocky foothills all across the plain, in long, brightly colored and balmy waves. Cut flowers are, of course, a major feature of the local economy; but in these parts it is perfume that counts for most.

Grasse. General view (above). Cutting flowers (bottom).

However, from the fourteenth century onwards Grasse was to become embroiled in the politico-religious feuding which, through a succession of sieges, occupations, looting and general destruction, was to bring about its decline. In the eighteenth century it recovered its prosperity, by means of its floral handicrafts and also its exceptional climate. Pauline Bonaparte, when separated from Prince Borghese, put the town on the map once and for all in 1807-1808, during a lengthy and tumultuous stay at a lavish mansion, located at 2 Boulevard du Jeu-de-Ballon. Every day she was carried in a sedan to contemplate the sweetly scented plain, at a point which soon became the garden of Princess Pauline, just above the palatial Rothschild property where

ries—are crowded together on high ground. The center of this picturesque district, with its narrow, steep, winding streets, crossed by stairs and arcades, is Place du Petit-Puy.

On this square the town hall is housed in the former bishop's palace, which still retains the lower parts of the original medieval structure, in particular a covered passageway with galleries, whose thirteenth century arcades support a loggia.

The other side of the square, the Cathedral of Notre-Dame-du-Puy, a very austere twelfth century building, which was consecrated in 1189, illustrates the slow, hesitant way in which Gothic was introduced to Provençal Romanesque. Its bright limestone is evidence of the powerful influence of Lombardy.

Curiously, the glover-tanners were the ancestors of the perfumers, on account of the fashion for scented gloves which was brought in from Italy during the Renaissance. In the sixteenth century Catherine de Médicis, who was extremely fond of perfume, sent the Florentine specialist Tombarelli to the region, with the task of distilling for her extracts of lavender and rosemary. In those days, these, together with orange, myrtle and lentisk, were the only local plants in use. In the seventeenth century, however, imports of Indian jasmine, Iranian roses and Italian tuberoses broadened the range of scents in use. Modern chemistry did the rest. In the eighteenth century a new process fixed the perfume on a fatty substance which could then be simply dissolved in alcohol.

In the nineteenth century extraction made it possible, by means of crushing the flower in hydrocarbons, to obtain after evaporation a concrete base for the «absolute» perfumes we know today. It is that same base which is now used in the composition of studiously prepared blends of scents.

Grasse. The Magagnosc district (above). Fountain on an old square (left). Following pages: the flower market.

THE COUNTRY-SIDE AROUND GRASSE

A host of gently rolling hills, covered with flowers and olive trees, lies between Grasse and the coast –a scented bucolic wonderland, rich with warm Mediterranean enchantment.

Each of the villages dotted about the landscape is an oasis of beauty and serenity, in lush and unspoilt natural surroundings.

The handsome houses of the village of Opio are scattered among the terraced olive groves and fields of flowers being grown for the perfume trade. The church, on which a little too much restoration work has been done, has lost all its charm. Visitors should, however, take a look at the superb residence of the Bishops of Grasse (seventeenth century), and especially a remarkable fourteenth century oil mill with its huge millstones.

Valbonne, surrounded by pine groves and scrub, derives its name from a Roman agricultural colony, Vallis Bona, established in the «good valley» of Grasse. In the late Middle Ages (1199) Cistercian monks founded a community here, building a curious village with a gridpattern layout as well as the church. All that has survived of this monastic venture

is a charming square bordered with arcades and shaded by elms, as well as an elegant belltower.

The most interesting piece of architecture in Valbonne is the church of Notre-Dame-du-Brusc, in the middle of the countryside, on a plateau which the Romans used as a graveyard for more than six centuries. The present church was built in the twelfth century over the remains of a rustic oratory of the sixth century.

From here we move on to Mougins, an old village, perched on a hill, of which Picasso was so very fond.

In the thirteenth century it was more important than Cannes or Vallauris, and ringed by powerful outer walls through which access was provided by monumental gates. Little now remains of all this, except segments of walls and a fortified entrance of the fourteenth century.

Apart from that, Mougins has merely the charm of its venerable streets, of its languid old houses and

An oil mill at Opio (facing page). View of Valbonne (above). At Mougins, an old fountain (left).

its Place de l'Ormeau, graced by a refreshing nineteenth century fountain.

A few miles away we come to two interesting chapels, nestling among the vegetation: Saint-Barthélemy, which has a curious octagonal layout, and Notre-Dame-de-Vie. In its early years, in the twelfth century, this charming place of worship, which is situated near a supposedly miraculous spring, was a hermitage of the monks of Lérins. For the most part the present building dates from the seventeenth century, though restoration work was also performed in the fifteenth century.

Three views of recent construction at Sophia-Antipolis and the church at Cabris (facing page). Saint-Cézaire-sur-Siagne: panoramic view of the mountain peaks surrounding the village (above) and a Romanesque chapel (right).

THE VILLAGES OF THE LOUP VALLEY

In order to reach the picturesque villages of the Loup Valley we must follow a winding and hilly route which is one of the most scenic of the Côte d'Azur hinterland.

Climbing the desolate and majestically wild hillsides of Caussol, the road reaches Gourdon La Sarrasine («the Saracen»), which stands on a rocky spur, at an altitude of nearly 2,500 ft. This is the supreme vantage point, a veritable aerie overlooking the Loup gorges. The old houses with their red tiled roofs are huddled around the castle of the Counts of Provence, built in the thirteenth century on the handsome ruins of a Saracen fort of the ninth and tenth centuries.

Arranged around a majestic ceremonial courtyard, the Moorish vaulted rooms have ornate ceilings which testify to the influence of the Tuscan Renaissance in the fourteenth century. A small museum of medieval art has been established there, as the village had become a favorite abode for artists and craftsmen. From the gardens which surround the castle there is a simply immense panoramic view.

Changing direction at the Bramantan bridge, the road follows some steep-sided gorges, passes the Saut-du-Loup, the turbulent Courmes waterfall, which is 45 ft high, and then the Saint-Arnoux hermitage, before reaching Pont-du-Loup, where the bridge which was destroyed in 1944 has never been rebuilt. Le Bar-sur-Loup is a typical Provençal village, whose concentric narrow streets center on a conical rocky spur.

The church, founded in the thirteenth century, but restored in the Gothic style in the fifteenth, has a huge altarpiece by Louis Bréa,

The village of Bar-sur-Loup (top, left). View of Gourdon and its fortress (top, right and right). Magagnosc (facing page, bottom).

consisting of fourteen panels. The majestic ruins of the castle of the Counts of Grasse are further enhanced by stately medieval towers built in the sixteenth century.

One's first sight of Tourette-sur-Loup comes as a real esthetic shock. Situated at an altitude of 1,300 ft, on a rocky plateau whose sheer sides fall away into the valley, the village stands resplendent with the feudal crown of its narrow houses forming the unbroken mass of a powerful defensive rampart.

Three square towers dominate this spectacular architectural ensemble, which we enter by passing through a fortified gate beneath a belfry. The most striking architectural feature of Tourette-sur-Loup, apart from its spectacular silhouette, is a fourteenth century single-nave church which is most noteworthy for its gilded carved wooden altarpiece and the presence, behind the altar, of a ritual stone slab belonging to a pagan sanctuary dedicated to Mercury which dates from the first century AD.

This delightful village has attracted a number of artists and craftsmen. Potters, weavers, engravers, sculptors and painters do their contemplative and creative work in the shadow of the romantic remains of the castle of the lords of Ville-neuve-Tourette.

Assorted views of the famous medieval village of Tourette-sur-Loup.

VENCE, SAINT-PAUL AND CAGNES

On its hilltop, at the foot of the grey and white cliffs of Les Baous, Vence rises from the midst of groves of olive and orange trees, and fields of flowers.

Set in a diadem of fawn walls, it has a truly proud bearing, and retains, at heart, a great deal of its medieval character.

Originally it was the capital of the Nerusi Ligurians, then an outpost of Caesar, and finally, by the name of Vintium, a colony of Augustus. Four centuries of Pax Romana brought it prosperity, before it was destroyed by the Lombards in 578. It thereafter vegetated until the departure of the Saracens in the ninth century, and was revived only when it once again became the seat of a bishop.

The ramparts, whose northern section is superb and still intact, date from the twelfth century, although they were considerably renovated and improved by François I, Henri II and Henri IV.

Access to the feudal town is guarded by several heavily fortified gates. In the center of the old town stands the eleventh century cathedral, which was built from Roman stone. Its Romanesque design, however, was remodeled a number of times over the years.

It is surrounded by a closely packed tangle of picturesque old streets, interspersed with tiny squares in the shade of occasional stairways and arches. On the Place du Frêne, situated at the foot of the walls, and graced by a giant and very ancient tree which is said to commemorate the visit of François I in 1538, we come to the impressive castle of the local feudal lords, which was restored in the seventeenth century. The massive square tower which looms above it, the sole remains of the original citadel, was built in the fourteenth century.

Beyond the monumental fortified Peyra Gate, the Place du Peyra, at the foot of the castle walls, stands on the site once occupied by the forum of the ancient city of Vintium. The elegant chapels of the Rosaire, the Pénitents Blancs and Sainte-Anne, all from the seventeenth century and located in a variety of historic parts of the town, contain works of art or are used as exhibition galleries.

The famous Rosaire chapel, attached to the order of the Dominican Sisters, was built in 1950 and decorated by Matisse with lively frescoes consisting of black strokes on a brilliant white ceramic background. The brightly colored stained glass windows cast an extraordinary soft light which contrasts with the ascetic plainness of the drawings.

Saint-Paul-de-Vence, another fortified village perched on its rocky spur a few miles away, has an even more striking silhouette. The military observatory of Saint-Paul-du-Var, on its natural bastion, was originally intended as a way of monitoring the frontier with Savoy. In 1868, after many upheavals and destructive episodes, peace eventually reached the small town. Thereafter it was able to relax and enjoy the rich scents wafting up from the plain, to gild its ancient stone in the sun and develop as an inspiration for artists.

Looking down over the Cagnes Valley, in an amphitheater of hills

Vence. Doorway of the cathedral (above). Facing page: overall view and the Peyra fountain.

*The village of Gréolières (above), the church
and some nearby ruins (below). Coursegoules,
deep inside the Baou (right).*

*Saint-Paul. Street along the ramparts (above)
and overall view (right). The courtyard
of the Maeght Foundation (top).*

strongly reminiscent of the landscape
of Tuscany, it slumbers behind its
ramparts, which have lost all of their
military purpose but which nonetheless are still very beautiful. Mandon,
the architect of François I, built these
defensive walls, which are still in
perfect condition, to serve as a loo-
kout over the nearby frontier of the
Var, which separated France from the
territory of the House of Savoy. Not-
withstanding its warlike appearance,
Saint-Paul-de-Vence has always been
a town with a poetic tradition, the
sophisticated and luxurious world of
troubadours and courtly love.

Within these remarkable ramparts
among the tangle of steep, winding
narrow streets, intersected from time
to time by stairways and vaulted passages, we find some handsome
medieval houses and squares which
have been famous far and wide on
account of their superb fountains. The
monumental gates are intact and still
very impressive, particularly the
Royal Gate and the Vence Gate, which
has its own stout defensive tower.

Painters from all over the world
have been fascinated by this wonderful place, as can be seen from the gal-
lery known as the Colombe d'Or
(Golden Dove), the celebrated restaurant which is a favorite rendez-vous
for artists, and the Maeght Foundation,
on Gardettes Hill. Founded in 1964

Cagnes-sur-Mer. The Hauts de Cagnes (top). Le Broc, a village in the Var Valley (facing page, bottom).

by the dedicated art collector after whom it is named, it is built in a most distinctive style, designed by José Luis Sers. All of the world's most talented artists have had their works shown here, in this inspired environment, which Malraux called «the antechamber to the supernatural».

On our way through Cagnes-sur-Mer we descend from the hill to the coast, as this curious town really consists of three attached but quite different parts. The historic district is situated on the Heights of Cagnes, which was the site of the original Ligurian settlement, on the rocky spur overlooking the marshes of the estuary. Then in the fifth century, it came to be occupied by the abbey of Saint-Véran, which had been restored by Charlemagne in 777, looted by the Saracens in the ninth century and finally restored by the monks of

Lérins in 1050 before being abandoned once and for all. The citadel of the house of Rainier-Grimaldi was also situated on the same high ground, from the fourteenth century to the Revolution, during which it was ransacked and the castle was sold. Converted into a princely residence in 1620, its majestic silhouette still towers over the old village. In 1946 the municipality installed in it an unusual Olive Tree Museum.

The old streets of the medieval town are enclosed within a rather rudimentary fortified wall, with crenellations but no bastion, dating from the twelfth and thirteenth centuries. Visitors enter through the monumental Ferrière (or Saint Paul) Gate, which was originally the only way into the town.

Down on the plain the fields of carnations, gladioli and roses pour

their scents into the air over the terraces and also over the Malvan and Cagne valleys. The new town, also known as Le Logis, which can be seen across the fields of mimosa and vines, would not be particularly interesting were it not for the famous Colettes estate, a few miles away. Auguste Renoir built the enormous house in 1908, in the middle of a hundred and fifty venerable olive trees, and lived there until his death on 3 December 1919. It can hardly be described as a museum, since it contains too few of the artist's works, but his restored studio makes a moving pilgrimage.

From the Colettes estate the road climbs back up the Cagne Valley, past fields of cultivated flowers, as far as La Gaude (820 ft) and then descends once more to Saint-Laurent-du-Var.

NICE

Visitors flock to Nice all year long, with the summer season prolonging the winter season, when there is an unbroken succession of exhibits, festivals and festivities.

Théodore de Banville thought that Nice was a "goddess stepping from the waves in a kiss of sunlight". He also remarked that "You may go to Nice for a week, and stay for a lifetime".

Having been "discovered" by the English in 1763, it was "colonized" by them thereafter practically without interruption, except for the harsh years of the Revolution and the wars of the Empire. And they certainly deserve full credit for this; after all, it took three days to get from London to Paris, and thirteen days, with over a hundred posting houses along the way, from Paris to Nice. The advent of the railroad, in 1865, greatly accelerated the growth and prosperity of Nice.

The site on which the modern city stands had been occupied since prehistoric times. The Lympia cave, which was buried during the construction of the new town, showed clear signs of human habitation dating back 400,000 years, while the Lazaret cave, at the foot of Mount Boron, had been an Acheulian settlement between the third and fourth ice ages.

Around 600 BC the Phoceans, from the coast of Asia Minor, settled on the rim of the Mediterranean. And it is quite certain that around 350 BC, at the foot of the Château promontory, there was a trading station and port of call of the Greeks of Marseille, known as Nikaia. It has been claimed that the name itself tells us about the circumstances of its foundation. Nike could be either the legendary «victory» over the Etruscans of Corsica in a naval battle for control of what is now the Côte d'Azur, or a water-nymph, a mythical goddess symbolizing the spring which enabled the trading station to survive.

While the Greeks were on the coast, at the Château, the Vendiantii Ligurians occupied the *oppidum* of Cimiez, two miles inland, in the fifth century BC. They in turn were replaced by the Romans, in 120 BC. The city, Cemenelum, admirably located on the Via Julia, which linked Rome to its Gaulish colonies, became the administrative capital of the region around the year 14. The fall of the Empire led to the disappearance of the ancient Cimiez, which in the fifth century had been raised to the status of a bishopric, in a Merovingian city. Throughout the Middle Ages it was poisoned by the schism in Provence and by the endless conflicts between the Kingdom of France and the House of Savoy, both of which sought to control it. Additional destruction was wrought by Spaniards, Austrians and even Barbary Turks. The great outbreak of the plague in 1631, which lasted seven months and wiped out the bulk of the population, thus compounded the military calamities and destruction inflicted on the city. With the exception of two brief periods of French rule, Nice remained under the control of Savoy until 1860.

«Niçois nationalis»' was very much in evidence throughout those turbulent times; for example, Catherine Ségurane, a kind of home-town version of the fifteenth century heroine Jeanne Hachette, defended the city against the Turks under Soliman and the soldiers of François I, who were allied against the House of Savoy. When two hundred galleys arrived in the Villefranche roadsteads on August 7 1543, bearing Ottoman troops under the famous Barbarossa, she galvanized the resistance of the people of Nice, who had taken up defensive positions at the Château. This strong and big-hearted washerwoman fought at the battlements, swinging her paddle with great gusto, and according to legend played a pivotal role in the defeat of the attacking force.

Nice is situated in a natural hilly amphitheater, against the majestic background of the Alps, on one of the most harmonious bays in the Mediterranean. Its climate, its seafront and the lushness of its vegetation make it one of the most

Panoramic views of Nice, seen from the Baie-des-Anges.

Nice. The Promenade des Anglais and the Hôtel Negresco (above).
Facing page: the Espace Masséna and the fountains (top).
The modern buildings of the Acropolis (bottom).

enchanting places to stay along the whole of the Côte d'Azur.

The resplendent seafront brought glory to Nice. It was here that rich English visitors began to settle, from 1731 onwards, in the Croix de Marbre district. In those days the coast was marshy and roads were very poor. In 1820 the Rev. Lewis Way hired a host of destitute and unemployed laborers to lay out a coast road along the shore, known at the time as *lou camin dei Angles*, two and a half miles of which, in 1932, became the famous Promenade des Anglais.

Sumptuous villas, stately mansions and palatial baroque hotels were built along the seafront, behind a fringe of palm trees. Alongside the world-famous Negresco, which was built in 1900 and has now been classified as a historical monument, there are other celebrated and elegant residences. These include the Villa Fultado-Heine (1787), where Princess Pauline Borghese stayed; Villa Giuglia, which was turned into a Mediterranean university center in 1933; and Villa Masséna (1900) which was donated to the city by the marshal's grandson. These buildings, all of which are in the lavish, ornate Belle Epoque style, stand over the Paillon, a small stream which formerly flowed through a marshy, reed-covered mouth into the Baie des Anges.

At the end of the promenade we come to the Château, a rocky headland towering over the sea from a height of 300 ft. This was once the acropolis of the Greeks. All that remains of it now is a bucolic pine grove, where recent excavations have brought to light the remains of the twelfth century Cathedral of Sainte-Marie. The Bellanda Tower, sole surviving part of a feudal castle which was completely razed in 1706, on the orders of Louis XIV, has been turned into a naval museum including weapons and models.

*Nice. Château Hill: Bellanda Tower
(above) and the park (left).
Facing page: view of the harbor
and the waterfront.*

Centuries ago, at the foot of this rocky spur, the road which ran between the bottom of the cliff and the south shore, was known as *rauba capeu*, or «hat robber», because of the strong winds common at that point. Now it is a picturesque boulevard. Lympia («pure water») harbor lies sheltered behind the promontory. It still bears the name of the first cove which served as a port of call for the Greek traders, in the shallow, marshy waters, where there was, however, a fresh-water spring. A real harbor was not excavated there until 1750.

The old town is situated around the Cathedral of Sainte-Réparate, on Place Rosetti, which is itself not particularly old (1650).

There are also a number of other interesting buildings, among them the seventeenth century church of Saint-Jacques, also known as the Gèsu, because it is an imitation of the Gèsu in Rome and is, like it, a Jesuit institution.

The Palais Lascaris, built in the seventeenth century in the grand style of the Genoese mansions of that period, is now a museum with highly varied collections, including ceramics and folk art. The palace is noted for the beauty of its high ceilings and its ornate stucco work.

In this old part of Nice the seventeenth century streets—where washing is hung out to dry from the windows, in the Italian style—weave a complicated web. Here between the sea and the castle we find the lively, bustling town of small shops, with homespun restaurants, sellers of *pan-bagnat* and craftsmen's stalls all trying to attract customers. And wherever one looks, pastel tones of plaster are evidence of Italian influence. A stroll around the streets, with no fixed plan—the best kind of all—will enable us to discover a clocktower, the former belfry of a Franciscan convent, or a 1850 mansion, now turned into a labor exchange, and, further on, one of the countless chapels dotted about the old town. Most of these were the

chapels of confraternities of penitents, which were so numerous throughout the region in the seventeenth and eighteenth centuries. With their membership based on social and professional categories, distinguished by the color of robes and hoods, they played an influential role in the life of the city.

The Black Penitents were the nobles, the White craftsmen and peasants, the Blue were property-owning townspeople and merchants, and the Red were seafarers and fishermen. Among these sanctuaries, the chapel of La Miséricorde, with its unusual oval layout, is a lavishly decorated Baroque masterpiece built in 1736 by Bernardo Vittore. Saint-François-de-Paule, the work of Guarini (1733), a

fine example of florid Niçois baroque, is more secular than religious.

The church of Saint-Augustin (seventeenth century) is noteworthy on account of an exceptional Pieta by Louis Bréa, the chief exponent of Niçois primitive painting in the sixteenth century.

Lastly, the marvelous flower market, at the end of the old town, behind the seafront, is a resplendent display of colors, scents and vitality.

There is also an abundance of

Facing page: one of the Italianate façades of the patrician dwellings in Nice.
The Fontaine des Tritons (above).
Views of the flower market.

Nice. The Salle Apollon, in the Acropolis (top).
The Château de l'Anglais (above).
Facing page: the Roman remains
at Cimiez (top) and the monastery (bottom).

museums all over Nice, ranging from the rather serious Museum of Natural History, dealing with the evolution of life on earth, to the most curious Museum of Molluscs, and including the Vieux-Logis, with its exhibits of the furnishings and everyday objects of past centuries. The most lavish is the Massénas Museum which presents the history of the county and some fine works of the Bréa school of primitive Niçois painting. The Chéret Museum, also housed in the splendor of an ornate Belle Epoque villa, displays a highly eclectic choice of classical painters and sculptors, Fragonard, Natoire and Sisley, next to Carpeaux, Rodin and Bourdelle.

The Arena Villa, built in the seventeenth century between the remains of the thermal baths and those of the amphitheater, contains some archeological collections and a remarkable Matisse Museum in which all the work done by the painter at his Cimiez studio are exhibited. In these canvases we can detect the changes wrought by the artist's discovery of Mediterranean colors and light. The astonishing Biblical Message Museum was built in 1972 by the architect A. Hermann to house the seventeen large canvases depicting the biblical message of Marc Chagall, painted over a thirteen-year period (1954-1967) with a powerful lyricism and a naïve enchantment.

The Cimiez Monastery rounds off our visit. After being awarded to the Franciscans in 1564, it was for many years subordinate to the nearby Benedictine abbey of Saint-Pons, whose buildings, now a military hospital, cover the nearby hill. The church, before which there stands a latticework cross of the sixteenth century, is a composite whole, combining a fourteenth century nave and a seventeenth century porch. The interior is illuminated by some fine works of Bréa (fifteenth-sixteenth centuries).

From the terraced gardens there is a magnificent view of the Nice coastline and the Château Rock, the only part of the city on which nothing has been built. To the rear, a mound covered with cypresses represents the oppidum of the Ligurians, the first inhabitants of ancient Cimiez. In the cemetery are the tombs of Raoul Dufy (1953) and Roger Martin du Gard (1958), near that of Matisse.

VILLEFRANCHE AND CAP FERRAT

The last part of the Riviera runs from Mount Boron in the west to Menton and Italy.

Here we are in the kingdom of sunshine, warm seawater and intensely blue sky and lush vegetation. Although tourism and real-estate development have made severe inroads along this part of the coast, it has managed to retain some picturesque historical sections which testify to its Italian past. The winding, indented and often sheer coastline is one enormous bed of flowers and plants, changing color from one season to the next–from the yellow of mimosas to the pink of laurels and the white of orange blossom. Amongst the modern concrete structures are a fairly large number of ornate and rather dated baroque buildings from the florid Belle Epoque period.

Palatial grand hotels and languid palm trees are the common denomi-

The old town and the fishing harbor (below).

nator of these seafront resorts, where luxury and the cultivation of a high-class image are often the sole response of local promoters to the majesty and splendor of the natural setting.

Between Nice and Menton the finely chiselled border of the coastline, bathed in an exceptional light, unfolds in a riotous display of color. The three corniche roads follow the contours of the rocky fingers which the mountains thrust out into the sea, providing a splendid view from various altitudes.

The low road along the coast is also the liveliest and the most heavily traveled, as it leads to all the seaside resorts and hugs the changing contours of the inlets, with their red rocks.

The road first passes around

Various views of Cap Ferrat. Following pages: the harbor at Saint-Jean-Cap-Ferrat.

Mount Boron, where we find the striking silhouette of the Saint-André fort, a fine example of sixteenth century military architecture, which so impressed Vauban that he decided to leave it standing.

Villefranche-sur-Mer, whose superb roadstead is very well sheltered from the wind, enjoys one of the best locations on the Riviera. Spread out in tiers over the rocky amphitheater at the edge of the bay, Villefranche has always been closely involved with seafaring.

For some strange reason, however, there does net seem to have been a Greek or Phenician trading station, or a Roman colony, at this remarkable spot. The first city was founded by Charles II of Anjou, Count of Provence and King of Sicily, in the early part of the fourteenth century as a duty-free trading port. This accounts for the name, *Cieuta franca*, later Villefranche, or "Freetown", which he gave it. Charles V stayed there in his galley the *Santiago*, from June 9 to 22, 1538. The town was a naval base and arsenal of the kings of Sardinia. The roadstead, which is 1,2 miles long and just over half a mile wide, with a depth of 80 ft, covers a total area of 860 acres. There is no better shelter for ships anywhere along the coast; indeed it can accommodate an entire squadron. The fishing harbor, though small, has remained lively and picturesque.

The old town, still intact within its fortified walls, stretches up the slopes leading to the middle corniche. Its dominant feature is the sixteenth century citadel, designed by Piovana, which, like the Saint-André fort and various other structures, earned such high praise from Vauban that he had it preserved.

With its covered lanes, one of which, known as the Rue Obscure, is a genuine tunnel, with its steep stairs, as well as the rustic and ancient façades of its houses, the medieval town really seems to be in something of a time-warp, worlds apart from the bustling crowds of tourists and the forest of smart masts in the harbor for pleasure craft. Yet a small Romanesque chapel, Saint-Pierre-des-Pêcheurs (St Peter of the Fishermen), once used as a warehouse for fishing nets, has been restored and handed over to Jean Cocteau in 1974 for restoration. The artist decorated it with scenes from the Bible, with bright colors and bold strokes.

Before coming to Beaulieu we have to take the road around the Cap Ferrat peninsula, which resembles the headland at Antibes.

It is also a rocky finger protruding into the sea, its lavish mansions discreetly hidden among its lush vegetation. A villa built between 1905 and 1912 at the narrowest point of the isthmus was donated in 1934 as a museum to the Academy of Fine

The headland of Cap Ferrat (above). The Villa Ephrussi de Rothschild (right) and its gardens (bottom).

Arts, by its owner, Mme Ephrussi de Rothschild.

Surrounded by an eighteen-acre park liberally strewn with statues, stone basins and small temples in the classical style, this rather astonishing place seems ill at ease in its Mediterranean setting; nonetheless it is definitely worth seeing.

Its eclectic collections which, though quite unrelated to the cultural climate of the Riviera, are in the best taste and of exceptional quality, include tapestries, oriental carpets, furniture, china, porcelain, objects from the Far East; paintings from Natoire to Sisley, including works by Renoir, Monet and Fragonard.

The road around Cap Ferrat itself is rather nondescript, passing some handsome mansions, the prototype of which is Villa des Cèdres, formerly owned by King Leopold II and now an elegant botanical garden, and a number of idyllic paths, such as the one which leads to Saint-Hospice Point; here an eighth century watchtower stands next a small chapel built in 1821 by the king of Sardinia on the site of an oratory where a hermit from Nice, Saint Hospice, lived in the sixth century.

Beaulieu-sur-Mer is sheltered by

Cap Ferrat. Gardens stretching up the hillside look down over the old harbor and a small pebble beach. The new harbor is reserved for yachts and other pleasure craft.

On Fourmis Point we come to the only local sight of any note, Villa Kerylos, which is the outcome of a most unusual venture. At the beginning of the century a wealthy amateur archeologist, Theodore Reinach, who died in 1928, commissioned the architect Emmanuel Pontremoli to recreate a Greek house. The resulting villa, a reflection of Greek art and a rigorous synthesis of its esthetic canons, is accurate down to the last detail. It is also decorated with superb originals ranging from the sixth century BC to the second century AD.

Eze-sur-Mer is merely the beach of Eze, the perched village which we shall come to later on the middle corniche. Its small beach of fairly large pebbles is situated at the foot of an imposing sheer rock face.

The highway and the railroad, which had hugged the shoreline so tightly as to make access to the sea difficult at times, now swings inland between Mala and Rognos points, opening up a broad and eminently usable coastal strip.

This area is occupied by Cap d'Ail, which is spread out over the western slopes of the Tête de Chien, behind which Monaco is situated. Besides its delightful natural setting, the small town, which was launched in 1879 by Baron de Pauville, has little to offer apart from an open-air theater adorned with mosaics by Jean Cocteau. The famous Monaco rock, however, is already visible in the distance, and we soon cross the symbolic frontier to enter the Principality, after the Ermitage Château.

Two views of Cap d'Ail (facing page). A villa in Beaulieu (above), and the nearby coast (right).

Monaco.
The Rock and the
castle (above).
Some views of the
old town (below).
At the entrance,
the coat of arms of
the Grimaldis
(facing page).

MONACO

One should take care not to confuse the historic town of Monaco, the almost mythical cradle of a most venerable dynasty, perched on its rock, with Monte-Carlo, the modern town and gamblers' paradise, set in its mountainous amphitheater.

The striking terrain of the rock was settled in the earliest prehistoric times, even before the Ligurians, who occupied the Italian coast, moved in there around the sixth century BC. They were driven out by the Phenicians of Tyr, who built a temple in honor of their god Melkart, the Herakles of the Greeks, on the rocky acropolis. The Phocean trading post, which became *Monoïkos*

(«one house») gave the name Monaco to the medieval community of the tenth century, ruled by a rich Genoese family, the house Grimaldi.

Restoring the ruins of the town, which had been devastated by Barbarians, Goths and Saracens, they built a massive and imposing citadel, which was occupied from the fourteenth century by Admiral Charles de Grimaldi.

In the course of four centuries

Monaco. The terraces of the prince's palace (above). The belltowers of the cathedral (below, left). The changing of the guard (below, right). The floodlit palace (facing page).

*Facing page: the harbor, between Monaco
and Monte-Carlo. Above: the entrance to the Casino,
the Hôtel de Paris and the Hermitage.
Below: the interior galleries of the Casino.*

All that remains of the fortress built in 1295 by Falco di Castello for the Republic of Genoa is the massive central bastion of Serravalle, and some curtain walls. The Tous-les-Saints Tower, the Oreillon Salient and the greater part of the outer walls date from the sixteenth century.

In the seventeenth century the citadel was converted into a palace, retaining the original external defenses and adding some superb terraced gardens and princely apartments endowed with great comfort, elegance and refinement.

Though looted and turned into a military hospital during the Revolution, it was restored and embellished by Albert I, who rebuilt its clock tower, and also by Rainier III, who added a south wing.

The formal courtyard, paved with white and colored pebbles, is majestically harmonious. A marble staircase, in the Fontainebleau style, leads to the reception rooms, which are remarkable for their painted ceilings and ornate stucco, as well as their magnificent collections of paintings and objets d'art.

The neo-Roman cathedral, made of white stone from La Turbie, was built between 1875 and 1884. It stands on the site once occupied by another place of worship, in the thirteenth century.

The Oceanographic Museum was founded in 1911 by Albert I, a pioneer of that branch of science, which in those days was in its infancy. It is one of the best endowed, most colorful and most active institutions of its kind in Europe.

At its furthest tip, towering over the bay, we come to the Saint-Antoine fort, built in the seventeenth century by Giraud, a pupil of Vauban. Built on the slopes of Mount Agel, it stands facing the hill on which Monte-Carlo is situated.

The famous Casino, shrouded in myth, is the most notable sight in Monte-Carlo, a bold and essentially vertical enclave bristling with luxury apartment buildings.

every conceivable vicissitude–assassinations, protectorates, annexations–happened to the rock, which was incorporated at the time of the Revolution to the French Republic, in 1793. The name Port-Hercule, which it was then given, restored the historical links between the Genoese fortress and the town's original deity.

In 1814 Talleyrand restored the rule of the Grimaldi dynasty over Monaco. Charles I, who also reigned over Menton and Roquebrune, failing to find a solution to his financial difficulties, and shying away from the easy remedy of levying taxes, had the brilliant idea of starting gambling houses there; these ancestors of the present-day Casino promptly attracted gamblers, tourists and prosperity to the Principality. This marked the beginning of the town's remarkable expansion and of its wealth.

The rock, which measures 110 by 875 yards, and towers over the sea from a height of 213 ft, is the administrative capital of this tiny kingdom, which is so small that there is practically only room for official buildings. The castle is a most impressive and picturesque structure.

Two views of Roquebrune.

CAP MARTIN AND MENTON

After Monte-Carlo we pass through Saint-Roman and Cabbé, the two tiny seaside resorts associated with the splendid perched village of Roquebrune.

Cap Martin, the last peninsula along the Côte d'Azur, is covered with pine and olive groves, among which assorted mansions lie hidden. A scenic corniche-type road runs along the east shoreline and even passes under a Roman triumphal arch before reaching Menton.

The natural setting of Menton is one of the most charming on the coast. Its most pleasant seafront is ringed by wooded mountains, with the Alps visible in the background. This paradise for all kinds of plant life, enjoying one of the finest climates in all of Europe, has lemons ripening on the trees, sheltered from the ravages of the mistral. It is hardly surprising, therefore, that this spot was inhabited in prehistoric times by a race similar to Cro-Magnon man, which came to be known as Grimaldi, from the name of the village on the Italian frontier where the caves containing traces of that settlement are located.

History has left no traces of the subsequent period until the twelfth century, when the village was known as Mont-Othon, in honor of its feudal lord, the Count of Vintimille. In keeping with the shifting politics of the coast, it changed hands repeatedly, passing into and out of the control of Genoa, Anjou, the house of Grimaldi, Emperor Charles V and France. Together with Roquebrune it was attached to the Principality of Monaco until 1860, when Prince Charles III, confronted with a massive vote in favor of French rule by the populace, sold the town to Napoleon III.

The palm-shaded streets of the modern town, spread out behind its resplendent seafront, are situated over the former riverbed of the Careï. Its main attraction is the Palais Carnolis, the former summer residence

of Prince Albert of Monaco, which has been at various times a casino, a private residence (until 1960) and lastly a museum of painting.

The old town is the most appealing part of Menton. Its façades, painted pink or yellow in the Italian style, lend a faintly old-fashioned charm which many visitors find quite irresistible. Situated on either side of the Place Saint-Michel, whose mosaic pavement, of black and white pebbles, dates from the time of the Grimaldis, the two churches of old Menton provide an ideal setting for the music festivals which are held there every summer. The church of

Saint-Michel is a seventeenth century baroque structure flanked by a bell-tower 164 ft tall. As for the chapel of the Pénitents Blancs, its Renaissance façade is adorned with highly classical statues.

Visitors would do well to take a stroll around the old streets, which are still quite lively, as they might come across some charming old houses or reminders of historical events.

The suburb of Garavan, towards the nearby Italian border, stretches out along the Salettes beach, with its harbor for pleasure craft. A number of famous people, drawn by the

simple and delicate gracefulness of the resort, built sumptuous mansions on the hills overlooking Menton: Katherine Mansfield's Villa Isola Bella (1920), and Villa Fontana Rosa, where the Spanish novelist Blasco Ibáñez, a true devotee of this town, lived from 1922 until his death in 1928.

The former casino, built in 1909 by Tersling, has become the focus of the cultural events which attract so many people to Menton. The most noteworthy of these is the Biennale d'Art, founded by Matisse, and dedicated, the first time it was held, to Raoul Dufy. Since then many other

Cap Martin (above, left).
Facing page: two views of Menton and the surrounding landscape.

artists, including Braque, Chagall, Dali, Miró and Picasso have received a similar international endorsement.

As a kind of local answer to the Carnival in Nice, Menton has its own, rather unusual, Lemon Festival. During Mardi Gras week, ever since 1930, between one and two hundred tons of lemons have been the star attraction of the festivities held in the Bioves gardens, to the greater glory of the region's produce.

*Menton. The Jardin
des Colombières and the Jardin
Exotique, on Garavan Hill.*

*Facing page:
a small square
and the stairs in the old town.*

The old town Menton directly overlooking the sea (left and below). Facing page: historic chapel with Italianate façade, dutifully preserved in front of an apartment block.

The Grande Corniche highway (above). Detail from a wall in Eze (below). Facing page: the village and, far down below, the beach of Eze. Following pages: two narrow streets in the village.

THE MOYENNE AND THE GRANDE CORNICHE

The Moyenne Corniche winds its way along the mountainside, hugging its capricious curves.

It provides an excellent view of the coastline, from a distance which makes detailed observation possible. Along its eighteen miles of highway we are treated to landscapes consisting only of sea, sun, rocks and flowers. There is only one village along the way, but it is one of the most remarkable on the Côte d'Azur.

Eze stands on top of a spectacular rocky spur 1,330 ft above sea level. Its houses, with their red tiled roofs huddled together, form a rampart of dry stone the whole length of the streets which climb the steep rocky slopes. Originally a Ligurian *oppidum*, this outcropping of stone, which towers over the indented coastline, was eventually settled by the Phenicians of Tyr, who built the temple of Isis after which the village is named.

After the customary geopolitical musical chairs, involving Ligurians, Romans and Saracens, the medieval village was elevated to the rank of county in 1592. Its ramparts were dismantled in 1700 by Louis XIV. The village, which consists of a maze of narrow, winding cobble-stoned streets, intersected by arches, stairs and vaulted passageways, has retained a genuinely medieval air. Unfortunately the church is recent, dating back

only to the eighteenth century; however, there is a small chapel of the Pénitents Blancs which was built in 1306. Although restored, it is still most appealing, its porch leading into a vaulted street. It contains some sixteenth century paintings, as well as a Spanish wooden figure of Christ from the thirteenth century. The Vierge des Forêts is another curious work; its name derives from the fact that the child Jesus is, most unexpectedly, holding a pine cone in his hands. The narrow streets of Eze, which have been largely given over to the arts and crafts, lead to the fourteenth century castle which was dismantled by order of Louis XIV in 1706. All that now remains of it is some proud but useless ruins which do, however, serve as a splendid belvedere for visitors.

Built in 1806 by Napoleon, the Grande Corniche more or less follows the path of the ancient Via Aurelia; it looks down majestically over the coast and the two other corniche roads from altitudes of between 1,300 and 1,640 ft. In fact its altitude makes it the most extraordinary route between Nice and Menton—and one which aroused the admiration of the novelist George Sand (1804-76). The visitor is treated to a succession of spectacular passes,

panoramas and viewing tables in a unique natural setting which includes the most beautiful landscapes along the Côte d'Azur.

The view of the feudal village of Eze from the Grande Corniche is particularly striking. Apart from these sweeping views and the exuberance of the ambient color and light, there are really only two points along this highway which deserve a visit, but both of them are exceptionally interesting.

La Turbie, which stands at 1,575 ft above Monaco, is a medieval village which clings to a rocky ridge. Originally founded in ancient times, this was the *alpis summa* of the Romans, which served as a border between Transalpine and Cisalpine Gaul.

The Romanesque church of La Turbie was replaced by the baroque structure in the purest Niçois style, built in 1777, which is visited today. It does, however, have a moving Pieta of the sixteenth century school of Bréa and an unusual Christ made of cedar.

The big attraction at La Turbie is the Trophée des Alpes. This massive ancient structure, also known as the Tour d'Auguste, comprises a solid base of cut stone consisting of two recessed levels. At one time the square base, each side of which measures 125 ft, used to support an elegant circular Doric colonnade, wholly within the tradition of the *tholos*. A giant statue of Augustus, shown receiving the submission of two prisoners, crowned the entire edifice, 164 ft above the ground.

Quite near La Turbie we come to the Madone de Laghet, the most famous shrine in the region. Having been restored in the seventeenth century, the chapel, which has a polychrome wooden statue of the Virgin Mary dating from 1632, quickly attracted pilgrims from all segments of society, including kings and commoners.

Two streets in La Turbie (left). Facing page: the church of Notre-Dame-de-Laghet (bottom, left) and the famous Trophée des Alpes, built by the Romans.

IMPERATORI·CAESARI·DIVI·FILIO·AVGVSTO
PONT·MAXIMP·XIIII·TRIB·POT·XVII
SENATVS·POPVLVSQVEROMANVS

THE HINTERLAND OF NICE

The hinterland of Nice is actually the gateway to the Alps, whose snowy peaks seem to gaze down tenderly on the first convulsions of the coastal valleys.

The gems of this area are its wonderful villages, which every visitor should make a point of seeing, no matter how great the detour. Though apparently identical, they are in fact all quite different.

In the extremely varied and often rugged terrain of the hinterland, the few inhabited points are all situated on high ground. These villages were perched in this way for purposes of defense and surveillance, but also in order to have the greatest possible exposure to the sun. The villages we see today are the direct descendants of the medieval settlements, which were themselves built on sites once

occupied by communities in ancient times.

Gorbio, at 1,480 ft, just above Roquebrune, is appealing particularly on account of its alleyways, connected by means of arcades and vaulted passages.

The ancient village of Sainte-Agnès, at 2,132 ft, is especially attractive, with the reddish stone of its houses blending perfectly into the sheer 150 ft cliff which towers directly over them. Apart from a few ruins, nothing now remains of the Saracen castle which once stood on this rocky spur, from which there are splendid panoramic views.

At 2,066 ft we come to the medieval village of Peille which overlooks the plain, in a wilderness of desolate beauty, just at the foot of towering cliffs. An elegant arcaded square with a baroque fountain leads into this striking village which has a large number of handsome Gothic façades. The church has retained its Romanesque nave from the twelfth century

The villages of Gorbio (facing page) and Sainte-Agnès.

141

THE ENCHANTING FRENCH RIVIERA

while the remains of a stout medieval castle stand guard over the sleepy hamlet, above the Faquin ravine.

Peillon, slightly lower down, at 1,233 ft, is also quite extraordinary with its houses clustered on top of a narrow, steep rocky spur. Everything about this village–its narrow streets, the façades and the fountain–is attractively integrated into the natural surroundings. The modest chapel of the Pénitents Blancs, from the fifteenth and sixteenth centuries, contains a handsome figure of Christ, some paintings and a number of interesting frescoes.

A brief side trip to L'Annonciade, on the road to Sospel, enables the visitor to discover a monastery snugly nestling among the pine and eucalyptus groves. It was built between the sixteenth and nineteenth centuries. The adjacent chapel, which dates from 1703, with its fine modern stained glass windows made by Jean Cavalier in 1964, is quite unrelated to the original chapel.

Sospel lies in the middle of a cultivated basin. This pleasant town is divided into two parts by the Bēvera river, on which the twin-arch bridge, from the eleventh century, still retains its toll tower.

Handsome and spacious houses with galleries surround the Place Saint-Nicolas, on the left bank; while in the center of the old town on the right bank, with its Gothic façades, we find the seventeenth century church of Saint-Michel, which contains some fine primitive works by the Bréa school of Nice.

Passing through L'Escarène, where we find once again a picturesque old village with its inevitable seventeenth century baroque church, one should also take the opportunity to go to Lucéram, another old village built on a rocky escarpment.

In ancient times a Roman road passed this way–the famous salt road between the Mediterranean and Turin, which was a source of power and prosperity. Here again we find the characteristic medieval atmos-

Views of Peille (top), Sospel (right and facing page, bottom) and Peillon (facing page, top).

142

phere, along the narrow streets; a fortified enclosure, with a huge fourteenth century tower; and a pompous transitional Gothic church, remodeled in the seventeenth century in the Italian rococo style with the addition of florid decorative work of questionable taste. Despite its appearance, the interior contains a number of treasures; most notably, some painted altarpieces of the sixteenth century Bréa school, and a number of beautiful ecclesiastical objects (a cross, an alabaster Virgin, a monstrance and a reliquary).

The medieval village of Contes, which stands at 295 ft on a rocky spur, looks like an island out of the past, surrounded as it is by modern housing. Apart from its traditional old houses and the customary Renaissance fountain, it contains some treasures of gilded wood from the sixteenth century, hidden within its sixteenth century church, which was disfigured in the nineteenth century by the addition of a rather unfortunate belltower.

The nearby village of Coaraze contains, in the origin of its name, *coua rasa*, or «bare neck», a reminder of the earliest Ligurian inhabitants in these parts, who, unlike the Gauls, used to cut their hair. Once again we come across old houses, a seventeenth century baroque church,

and, above all, the small chapel of Saint-Sébastien, with the remains of some frescoes from the sixteenth century.

Tourette-Levens was a perched village, standing on top of a rocky spur. In the nineteenth century its inhabitants abandoned it, in order to settle at its feet. Some ruined houses can still be seen, as well as a single tower from the medieval fortress, which has now become part of a private dwelling.

The tiny medieval village of Castagniers still has some remains of its original fortified walls and a number of old houses, surrounding a ruined castle.

The illustrations of this book were supplied by the photographers of the following agencies:
Atlas, Pix, Scope and Vloo, except those on p. 11 (top) and 12 (bottom), respectively from Royer/Explorer and Philippon/Explorer.
The illustrations on the cover are from Lenars/Explorer, Jalain/Explorer, Giraudon/Explorer and Philippon/Explorer.

Achevé d'imprimer en avril 1995 sur les presses
de l'imprimerie Bona en Italie
Printed in Italy
ISBN : 2-83-070111-9